TAKE COMMAND OF YOUR FUTURE

- Make things happen!

ROBERTA CAVA

Copyright © 2013 by Roberta Cava

All rights reserved. No part of this work covered by the copyrights hereon may be reproduced or used in any form or by any means - graphic, electronic or mechanical, including photocopying, recording, taping or information storage and retrieval systems - without the prior written permission of the publisher.

Take command of your future

Make things happen!

Roberta Cava

Published by Cava Consulting

cavaconsulting@ozemail.com.au

Discover other titles by Roberta Cava at
www.dealingwithdifficultpeople.info

National Library of Australia

Cataloguing-in-publication data:

ISBN 978-0-9923579-3-1

BOOKS BY ROBERTA CAVA

Dealing with Difficult People
(22 publishers – in 16 languages)

Dealing with Difficult Situations – at Work and at Home

Dealing with Difficult Spouses and Children

Dealing with Difficult Relatives and In-Laws

Dealing with Domestic Violence and Child Abuse

Dealing with School Bullying

Dealing with Workplace Bullying

What am I going to do with the rest of my life?

Before tying the knot – Questions couples Must ask each other Before they marry!

How Women can advance in business

Survival Skills for Supervisors and Managers

Easy Come – Hard to go – The Art of Hiring, Disciplining and Firing Employees

Human Resources at its best!

Time and Stress – Today's silent killers

Take Command of your Future – Make things Happen

Human Resources Policies and Procedures

Employee Handbook

Belly Laughs for All! – Volumes 1 to 4

Wisdom of the World – The happy, sad and wise parts of life

That Something Special

Retirement Village Bullies

ACKNOWLEDGEMENTS

My special thanks to the brave people who were willing to bare their souls and tell their stories so that others could benefit from their experiences.

I'd also like to extend my thanks to the Canadian Mental Health Association who allowed me to quote directly from several of their brochures and WIN House (Women in Need) for allowing me to quote from F. Cearns brochure WIFE ASSAULT Hurts all of us, as well as Faye Wiesenberg of the Alberta Career Development and Employment Branch, who offered career-counselling advice.

DEDICATION

Dedicated to all the people who are in the process of learning how to take command of their futures. Chapter 7 is dedicated to my parents, Bob and Mabel Hastie who gave me a happy, secure child- and adulthood. This wasn't appreciated until I learned about the hideous childhoods some have been forced to endure.

TAKE COMMAND OF YOUR FUTURE

- Make things happen!

Table of Contents

CHAPTER ONE - *What's holding you back?*   13

     Are you 'stuck?'
     How well do you like yourself and your lifestyle?
     What's holding you back?
     Handling criticism and disapproval
     Fear of Failure
     I should have ... If only ...
     Indecisiveness
     Dependency
     Forgiving others
     Inflexibility
     Can't say no
     Fear of success
     Self-concern
     Setting expectations

CHAPTER TWO - *Where do you want to go?*   35

     Where do you want to go?
     Dreams can become a reality with goal setting
     Positive/negative goals
     Goal clarity
     Life Inventory
     Using your potential
     Criteria necessary for successful goal setting
     Lifetime and career goals
     Why is planning necessary?
     Sample good and bad goals
     Guidelines for setting personal goals

CHAPTER THREE - *How to overcome negative tapes*   **41**

    How do we get negative tapes?
    Harmful negative labelling
    How to remove negative tapes
    Constructive criticism

CHAPTER FOUR - *Setting career goals*   **57**

    Guidelines for setting career goals
    Reasons people end up in the wrong jobs
    Planning a career
    Mid-life career change
    Have you plateaued [in a rut?]
    Get ready for that promotion
    Goal Setting Plan
    Driving and Restraining Forces
    Rules for brainstorming
    Using the goal setting plan
    Putting the goal plan into action

CHAPTER FIVE - *How do I change my approach to life?*   **75**

    Mazlow's Hierarchy of Needs
    Make things happen
    Rate your self-esteem level
    How to improve your self-esteem
    How do I turn things around?
    You can't change the past, only the future
    Can I do it alone?
    The importance of friendships
    The technique of feedback
    How to give and receive compliments

CHAPTER SIX - *How can I become a more positive-thinking person?*   **95**

    How to maintain control during negative situations?
    You and your bad mood
    Positive vs. negative thinking
    How to deal with whiners, complainers and bellyachers
    Are you a positive/negative thinker?

Signs of having a negative attitude
Becoming a positive thinker
Imagination
The ability to visualise
Two magic questions

CHAPTER SEVEN - Dealing with manipulation   *111*

Manipulating others
Positive and negative manipulation
Game Playing
Passive Resistance
Indirect Aggression

CHAPTER EIGHT - Overcoming your past   *131*

Dysfunctional homes
Child abuse
How to keep the cycle from repeating itself
Wife battering
How to stop wife battering and child abuse
Adult rape victims
Battling spouses
How to resolve battles between spouses
Dealing with divorce
A man for every woman, a woman for every man
Are you still blaming others?

CHAPTER NINE - How to deal with your negative emotions   *149*

Early signs of emotional problems
Getting over the Holiday 'blues'
Tensions - how to live with them
How to handle a panic attack
Anger - the mystery feeling
How do you handle anger?
Repression of anger
Techniques used to handle anger
Heal thyself

CHAPTER TEN - *Turning things around*   *171*

    Using abilities
    Taking risks
    How can I improve my risk-taking?
    How you appear to others
    Obtaining inner peace
    Don't worry, be happy

CHAPTER ELEVEN - *How to be a winner*   *187*

    Success
    How do winners differ from losers?
    How to tell a winner from a loser
    Putting it all together

Bibliography   *193*

Career Counselling   *195*

INTRODUCTION

Command: To have or exercise direct authority; the ability to control.

- Are you just drifting through life spending one day after another just plodding through life?
- Have you forgotten how to channel your energy towards what YOU want in life?
- Do you just 'go with the flow' or let others decide where your life is heading?
- Do you allow outside forces to exercise direct authority and control over your life?
- Do you exist, rather than live and let situations or other people influence how and when your life progresses?
- Have you found yourself thinking; *'Is this all there is?'*
- Is life so boring that you hate getting up in the morning?

Most people aren't even aware of how they're wasting their lives. They get in a rut and stay there or make feeble stabs at changing their lives. The least kind of opposition sends them scuttling back towards their safety net of sameness. These people hate getting up in the morning, because there's not much that's exciting or stimulating in their lives. One day is just like another and the future's likely to be the same.

These people need a jolt to get them living again. Just as a heart-attack victim needs a jolt of electricity to get their hearts re-started, these people need a jolt of reality to put them back into the land of the living.

I wrote this book to help people see how important it is for them to take command of their future. It's written for people who find the following feelings and ideas controlling their thoughts:

- I can't do anything to change my life.
- Everybody else has more than I do!
- If only ...
- I should have ...

- Depressed or feeling low nearly all the time, even consider suicide,
- Feeling that nothing is worth doing,

Do you show behaviours such as:

- Being afraid to face the possibility of failure.
- Being unwilling to share material possessions.
- Repeatedly not being able to sleep.
- Permanently tired and lethargic. Find it hard to wake up in the morning - even after a good night's sleep.
- Worrying excessively about everything and are very apprehensive of the future.
- Afraid to make decisions whether they're large or small.
- Spending a lot of time imagining how matters could be - living in another world.
- Worrying excessively about minor physical ailments.
- Letting others make decisions - even small ones,
- Being unable to do activities on your own.
- Procrastinating and putting items off indefinitely.

Or do you use such expressions as:

- *'I'm not as smart as my brother.'*
- *'Can't I do anything right?'*
- *'What a klutz I am, that's three times I've done that wrong.'*
- *'How dumb/stupid can I be?'*
- *'I ought to know better.'*
- *'Sometimes I wish I'd never had kids.'*
- *'Why can't I be more like ...'*

Or is your anger shown in such ways as:

- Yelling at or blaming others.
- Being quarrelsome - continually or repeatedly - for almost no reason at all.
- Verbal abuse - sarcasm or ridicule.
- Using physical violence.
- Giving threats to others.
- Indulging in temper tantrums or angry outbursts beyond reason.
- Giving others 'the silent treatment' or withdrawing from them.
- Denying or ignoring what's really happening.

- Vandalism or sabotage.
- Alcoholism or drug abuse.

If any of the above feelings, thoughts or behaviours describes you or anyone you deal with, please read on.

Take Command of your Future

CHAPTER ONE

WHAT'S HOLDING YOU BACK?

'Good times become good memories.
Bad times become good lessons.'

Are you waiting for something external to change life's events for you? Are you expecting big brother, your company or society to 'look after you?' If you are - stop doing it. If you want something, go after it; don't expect it to come to you. Once I learned this philosophy, I found that my lot in life improved one thousand per cent. No longer do I expect situations to happen to me - I make them happen. You too can do this, if you're willing to put in the time and effort it takes to make it happen.

Use the expression *'If it's to be - it's up to me.'* This way, YOU control your future - not others.

'The future belongs to those who believe
in the beauty of their dreams.'

Are You 'Stuck?'

When people drift through life rather than controlling it, I think of them as being 'stuck.' They'll remain stuck where they are unless they do something to change their lives. For example:

Darren

Darren is a good-looking 36-year-old single man. He works in a dead-ended position with little challenge and opportunity for advancement. His workmates are similar. The most important topic within their group is, *'Who won the football game last night?'*

Darren frequents expensive nightclubs [that he can ill afford] with the hope that he will meet the 'right' woman. Successful women who are climbing their own corporate ladder are the ones that attract him. Initially he can make them believe him when he tells them that he holds an important position in a company. Soon he gives himself away and the women refuse to see him again [mainly because of his lying.]

He can't understand why he can't 'score' with the ladies. He doesn't understand that he sets himself up to fail by his game playing. Darren will remain 'stuck' until he changes his approach with women, looks for a more compatible mate and stops trying to be something that he's not.

Marcia

Marcia is a working single mother of a hyperactive son who drives her to distraction. Her energy level is at the opposite end of the scale to her son, and she finds it extremely difficult getting through her day.

She's tired at night, so when he whines and complains, she gives him what he wants which just encourages the negative behaviour of the child. Often what he wants is junk food. Marcia hasn't taken the time or the energy to find out that the hot dogs and cheesies she's allowing him to eat, add to his hyperactivity. Both she and her son are 'stuck' and will remain so until outside influences change the situation.

Marilyn

Marilyn's job is in jeopardy, and she's taken action by applying to over one hundred positions. She can't understand why potential employers reject her every time. She has a high school education and has worked for twenty years in clerical positions. This alone has not held her back from getting a new position. What's holding her back is her refusal to make any effort to upgrade her knowledge and keep up with office technology. Although her present company is using computers for most of its data entry, she has refused the training offered to her.

Right now, she's applying for supervisory positions, because she believes her twenty years in a clerical position have given her valuable experience. Unfortunately, she hasn't taken any courses to prepare for that new role. Marilyn is 'stuck' and will remain so, until she assesses the skills, she's really offering potential employers.

Phil

Phil has been overweight most of his life and although he spends his life dieting, he fails to keep off his excess weight. He's divorced, with grown children but is lonely and seeks female companionship. A friend told him about a dating service he had tried that had introduced him to five suitable women. Phil decided to apply himself. He described the kind of woman he was looking for but obtained the name of only one woman.

He complained to the dating service about this. He was dismayed to find that most of the women who fitted his qualifications, had stipulated they would not consider dating someone who smoked, an obese man or one with a 'beer belly.' Their reasoning was that if he didn't care enough about his own appearance and health, how could he care about the women he would meet. They were also reluctant to meet someone who was a prime candidate for diabetes or could die from a heart attack or stroke at an early age. Phil refuses to take these reasons at face value and act by losing weight and quitting smoking. He's 'stuck' where he is and will stay there unless something external changes his situation.

Jake

Jake could never understand why people weren't friendlier with him. If he was to describe himself, he would likely state, *'I'm tall, dark and handsome with a gift of the gab. I'm full of fun and the life of the party.'*

Jake doesn't comprehend that others see him as a person, so taken with himself and his successes that conversation seldom strays from discussing himself and his exploits. Although he's attractive, he soon turns off others with his 'holier than thou' attitude. Besides this problem, he's prone to using sarcasm on others, which has alienated many of his former friends.

Jake fails to realise that he lacks communication skills [mainly the ability to listen and understand other's feelings.] Jake is 'stuck' and will continue to lose friends unless he changes his attitude and behaviour towards others.

Margaret

Margaret is a quiet, timid woman in her late thirties who lives with her ailing mother. She realises that life is passing her by but doesn't act to do something to change her life. She spends her evenings and weekends caring for her mother. During the day an aide comes in to keep an eye on her mother [who has a tendency to wander.] Lately her mother's condition has deteriorated. Her doctor explained that her mother has Alzheimer's disease and suggested that she put her mother in a nursing home.

Margaret's two brothers refuse to contemplate this alternative but refuse to consider having their mother live with them. They explain that their first responsibility was to their families and that Margaret should be ashamed of herself for 'abandoning' their mother. Neither brother offers Margaret many breaks from caring for her mother. Because of this, Margaret's opportunity of socialising with men is nil.

Margaret allows her brothers to make her feel guilty, so she puts off changing her life. She's 'stuck' where she is until she decides that she should have and deserves a life of her own.

Grace and Jim

Grace is always after her husband Jim to get a better, higher paying job. Both earn about the same salary. Jim hates his job but can't see a way out. He'd like to become an electrical engineering technologist but thinks he can't afford to take two years off to get the training he requires.

At thirty years of age, he feels trapped in a catch-22 position. His wife is after him to get a better job: to get a better job, he needs to go back to school. She explains that they can't afford for him to do that, and he shouldn't expect her to support them while he completes his studies. To add to his woes, his marriage is becoming shaky.

Instead of acting on what he believes would be the best for him [getting a student loan and going back to school] he remains 'stuck' by taking a higher-paying job in his existing field.

Susan and Bob

Susan and Bob have been trying for five years to have a baby. Susan has had all the necessary tests and finds that there's no reason she shouldn't conceive. Bob refuses to be tested, saying it can't be his fault.

Susan's been hinting about adopting a baby, but Bob strongly resists. He says, *'If we can't have our own baby, I don't want any.'*

They'll remain 'stuck' unless they're lucky enough to conceive on their own.

Sally and Fred

Sally and Fred argue every year about where they'll spend their holidays. She likes to visit warmer climates like Hawaii or

Queensland in the winter months. Fred prefers to go camping and fishing in the summer, away from crowds. Every year they spend considerable time and energy arguing about where they'll go that year. They've contemplated having separate vacations and the marriage is showing signs of weakening.

One year they stayed home and spent their time building a fence rather than have one or the other unhappy. This couple hasn't learned to negotiate and compromise and will remain 'stuck' until they do.

Agnes and Dennis

Agnes and Dennis had an ongoing battle about getting the household chores done. Agnes worked as a real estate agent, so often had to work in the evenings. This often meant that dinner had to be fast food and the dishes left until she returned from showing homes to prospective buyers.

She would seethe when she returned late in the evening. She'd find a kitchen exactly as she had left it and her husband engrossed in watching television. She complained every time this happened, but nothing changed. On the evenings when she did not have to show a home, she had to prod Dennis to help her.

Agnes and Dennis are 'stuck,' and won't resolve this problem until they act. [By the way, the solution is that nobody in the home, including children, should be allowed to relax, until ALL the work is finished, be it doing dishes, shopping, cutting the grass or doing the laundry.]

Could your story be similar to any of the above? Are you 'stuck' by inactivity? Are you waiting for something external to change your life? If so, you [like the people identified above] will stay 'stuck' until you change your approach and take command of your future. It's better to try and fail, than to be afraid and do nothing.

> *'I look to the future because that's where I'm going to spend the rest of my life.'*

How well do you like yourself and your lifestyle?

How do you really feel about yourself and your lifestyle? Using the following scale, rate yourself with each of the following statements:

4 - if the statement is totally true

3 - if it's mostly true

2 - if it's partly true

1 - if it's hardly true

0 - if it's not true at all

1. I enjoy waking up in the morning.
2. I'm usually in a good mood.
3. Most people like me.
4. When I look in the mirror, I like what I see.
5. If I were a member of the opposite sex, I'd find me attractive.
6. I'm intelligent.
7. I enjoy my work.
8. There aren't many things about myself I'm ashamed about.
9. I feel comfortable about the number of my friendships.
10. I have plenty of energy.
11. I'm mainly an optimistic person.
12. I can laugh at my mistakes.
13. If I could live my life over, there isn't much I'd change.
14. I'm an interesting person.
15. I'm happy with my love life.
16. I'm still growing and changing.
17. Other people care about me.
18. There's nobody quite like me.
19. There's not much I'd change about my appearance.
20. I'm a kind person.
21. I don't have any regrets about my existing lifestyle.
22. The people I care about, value my opinion.
23. I'm not afraid to express my feelings.
24. I feel comfortable in a conversation.
25. I can make of my life whatever I want.
26. There aren't very many people I'd trade places with.
27. I've led an interesting life.
28. I like what I'm doing.
29. I like where I live.
30. Nothing's too good for me.

To improve the quality of your life, work on the items you rated 0, 1 or 2.

What's Holding You Back?

Do you allow others to make decisions for you? Some people never learn how to be assertive or to stand up for themselves. Inexperienced in the art of getting their own needs met, they allow others to manipulate them. They're unable to make decisions that support their own wishes, values and feelings. The result is they feel bad about themselves without knowing why. Learning how to satisfy their own needs while remaining sensitive to those of others can help them enjoy a healthier, satisfying life.

It's vital for individuals to understand from childhood that it's okay to express their wants and needs, providing they're not infringing on the wants and needs of others. The child who has a strong sense of his or her own value by the time s/he attends preschool, will usually get along well with other children. Parents must accept the child, as s/he is, not how they want or expect him/her to be. Nor should they compare their children to either siblings or other children.

Parents give encouragement to their children by giving them permission to express both their positive and negative feelings without reprisal. The children might need to be taught how to vent their anger and frustration in a positive way. They should be encouraged to make 'I' statements: 'I feel, I think, I believe' and understand there is a relationship between personal independence and assertiveness.

Some learn to rely on others to meet their needs instead of assuming responsibility themselves. This can often be the coddled 'baby' of the family, who is cared for not only by the parents but by older siblings as well. These children need to take control of their lives and take the consequences for their actions.

As children grow up, they may have difficulty keeping out of trouble - yet keep their friends. They need to set boundaries between what they will and will not do and follow those guidelines when they're faced with temptation. Children who grow up being non-assertive, often feel hurt and disappointed with their relationships when they become adults.

Handling Criticism and Disapproval

Most of us react instinctively to criticism. Our defence mechanisms rise, and we prepare to defend ourselves. Next time someone criticises you, force yourself to listen calmly to what they have to say before reacting. You'll likely find that there is some truth in what they're saying:

1. Control your thoughts and behaviour. [Essential for keeping your cool under fire.]Don't retaliate. Turn off your defence mechanism. Instead, use your energy to listen carefully to their comments.
2. Ask for specifics if criticism is vague.
3. Confirm your understanding of the problem [using paraphrasing].
4. If the criticism is valid, apologise. Let them know what steps you'll take to correct the behaviour or problem. Realise mentally that this error or problem is part of life and that you shouldn't expect perfection from yourself. Just strive not to repeat this error or cause the problem again.
5. If the problem or behaviour they're criticising is not your fault, defend yourself with facts, not emotions.

If you feel that others are trying to manipulate you - say so. Instead of feeling you have to please others who criticise you and want you to do tasks their way, say, *'Thank you for pointing that out to me.'* This negates the need for you to seek that person's approval or discuss why you did what you did. This way, whatever they think you should do, has no effect on you, unless you let it. You're free to continue doing tasks your way.

When others show disapproval, fight the temptation to start a sentence with the word 'I.' Instead use the word 'you' and describe how you think the person is feeling, responding or behaving.

For example, you note that a close friend is not agreeing with you and is even getting angry. Rather than defending your ideas, respond by saying, *'You're getting upset because you feel that I shouldn't think the way I do.'* This helps you know that the disapproval belongs to the other person - not you.

Non-assertiveness can cause the following fears to surface:

Fear of Failure

Fear is the most paralysing of all emotions. It can stiffen the muscles and stupefy the mind. Have you ever wondered why some people are unafraid to try things you wouldn't have the courage to try? Why is it that others have no problem switching from a very satisfactory job to a better [yet riskier] one? Why do others get married and have a family or go into business for themselves and yet these situations immobilise you?

Join the crowd. We're all afraid of something, which stems from our lack of trust in our ability to handle new situations. If you find yourself worrying about something, ask, *'What am I avoiding now by using my valuable energy with worry?'* The best antidote to worry is action.

Self-confidence and decisiveness often mark leaders in the world. A willingness to take chances, a solid faith in their ability to cope with just about any problem, are characteristics of winners.

As long as you're growing and changing, you'll experience fear. You'll feel fear whenever you're in unfamiliar territory - but that's normal. Getting rid of the fear is simply a matter of doing something about it and overriding the feeling of helplessness that may accompany it.

Fear of failure is very often the fear of someone else's disapproval or ridicule. Failure is someone else's opinion of how certain acts should be completed. Their perception of what's the right way to do something may differ widely from yours. Neither is wrong. Should a person not succeed at a particular endeavour, they have not failed as a person. They've simply not been successful at that particular event, at that particular moment.

'Without failure we learn nothing.'

Some shun experiences that might bring failure and avoid anything that doesn't guarantee success. They often turn down excellent opportunities but can't explain why they've done so. Or they explain, *'If I was sure I could swing it, I'd try. But ...'* if you have this happen to you, ask yourself, *'Why am I not taking this opportunity?'* Is fear of failure holding you back? Or is it a lack of money, connections, time or possibly anticipated family problems? Learn to analyse why you're being your own worst enemy. Then, decide from time to time, to bite off more than you're sure you can chew.

Mountaineers have all been in the situation where they get themselves into a position where they can't back down; they can only go up. Take the plunge occasionally where you know you'll have to deliver - or else. Unless you're hopelessly in over your head - you'll deliver. You can't acquire the trait of extending yourself to the utmost overnight. Confidence is a cumulative feeling. There will likely be setbacks and disappointments, but:

> *'Someone who tries to do something and fails,*
> *is a lot better off than the person who tries to do nothing*
> *and succeeds.'*

I know people who've sat on the fence wailing about their problems so long, they're afraid to get off and begin living. I call them Mugwumps. Mugwumps are those who have their mugs on one side of the fence and their wumps on the other. They've got to get off that fence and get on with their lives!

These people don't comprehend that they're putting themselves under more and more stress the longer they're on that fence. *Not* deciding becomes more stressful than deciding. Think of it - when you had a tough decision to make, wasn't it stressful? Do you remember the relief you felt when you finally took the step and made a decision? The tension goes somehow. Fence sitting is very draining as people mentally bounce from one solution to another, without deciding which decision is right. All you get from sitting on a fence is slivers!

If we offer these people promotions, they automatically assume they're incapable of handling them. They think of every situation where they couldn't possibly measure up. They'll often turn down a promotion because of these fears. Unfortunately, if they *do* accept the positions [and still have the negative feelings] they're probably setting themselves up to fail.

If you accept a promotion, you may have misgivings about taking it but know you must deliver or else. Unless you're hopelessly unqualified - you will deliver. Your pride, your competitive instinct and your sense of obligation will see to it that you do. Certainly, there'll be setbacks and disappointments; courage in itself is no guarantee of success.

I should have ... If only ...

Many people spend their lives reliving the past. They get into a mental rut that concentrates on what was, rather than what will be. Many of their comments start out with the prefaces, *'I should have ...'* or *'If only I could ...'*

Here's a story of a woman who has used those two prefaces for most of her life:

Celia married and stayed at home with her four children. She suffered from severe depression but did not receive professional help for it. Suddenly, at the age of 43 her husband Roger told her that he wanted a divorce because he wanted to marry someone else. Celia had not been aware there was trouble in the marriage, nor that her husband had been cheating on her. She had been so wrapped up in herself, that she had not seen the warning signs.

Celia was grief stricken and was unable to fully cope for the next ten years of her life. She leaned heavily on her teen-aged children who, in a way brought themselves up most of the time and looked after her needs, as well as their own. Her children loved her, but because she seldom gave them any guidance and was prone to complaining, her children lost respect for her. Her youngest son Bill drifted through life doing as little as possible around the home and simply put in time at school.

Five years after her husband left her, Celia realised that financially she would have to work, so applied for a part-time position as receptionist. Her hours of employment were unusual because she worked from six till ten in the morning. Because of these early hours of work, she found she had to cut her evenings short and was often in bed before nine o'clock. She seldom dated for two reasons. She still couldn't forget her husband and the thought of having an affair or being intimate with another man went against her beliefs as a strong Roman Catholic.

One of her friends introduced her to a man called Albert. The two of them hit it off right away. Both were racquetball lovers, liked quiet evenings at home and hit it off right away. This friendship continued for several years. Albert wanted Celia to marry him, but she kept putting him off refusing to make a commitment. She confided in her female friends that she felt that the magic was missing in their relationship and that he was too unsophisticated. They eventually broke up. Celia then spent her time working, visiting her grown children and female friends.

Celia had extreme mood swings. She could be on top of the world one hour and in the depths of despair the next. Her depressions were so severe that they influenced everything she did. She spent most of her energy railing over how her life had been. Most of her sentences began with the statements, *'If only ...'* Or, *'I should have ...'* Or, *'Why didn't I do something with my life earlier.'*

One of her friends is a trained counsellor who tried desperately to help Celia solve her problems and change her negative attitude into a positive one.

For some reason Celia surrounded herself with positive-thinking friends, who tried their best to convince Celia that it wasn't too late to try something new. Unfortunately, Celia kept comparing her life to that of her successful female friends who were high achievers and set reasonable goals for themselves. She insisted that others were more important than she and related her own lack of fulfilment to something outside herself. She didn't understand that there's nothing wrong with appreciating others' accomplishments. But it did become a problem when she modelled her behaviour on their standards, not her own.

Celia learned how to set goals for herself, but normally stopped trying before she achieved them. She always had a reason for quitting. It's unlikely that Celia will change her way of living unless she receives professional counselling. Her friends hope that she will do this for herself. In the meantime, her friends' patience at her inactivity towards helping herself, is alienating her from their strength.

Celia will likely lose her positive-thinking friends soon unless she changes her approach to life, which in turn will likely make her even more depressed.

Remembering the past can be a painful, counterproductive occasion. Using twenty-twenty hindsight, you can probably see exactly where you went wrong - on a job interview, in a love relationship or in moving to a new city. These thoughts can cause immobility and make a person remain in the negative rut they're in. They feel depressed, uneasy and even out of control of their life. If this sounds familiar, you've probably fallen into this trap. This kind of thinking has become a habit, but habits can change. In this case it will take more than a little effort, but you can do it!

Try to stop thinking of life in black or white terms. There are many grey areas in between. Some feel that if they fail at something, that they're a failure as a person. Others are perfectionists who believe that if they don't perform flawlessly, they'll disgrace themselves. Many set complex goals that would be impossible to reach. Because it's impossible to be perfect, they're always dissatisfied with themselves.

Others give up too soon. At the first sign of trouble, they convince themselves that they weren't meant to succeed at something. Instead of trying another avenue or another way of doing something, they quit trying. Many pass the buck, stating something or someone made them fail. By blaming others for their failure, they feel they can absolve themselves of its responsibility. Many make a mountain out of a molehill and magnify the expected results of making a mistake. If a real calamity were to happen - they give up completely.

These people are constantly comparing themselves to others. They compare their successes, status and position to others. They believe that people like others more than them - anything they feel puts them in a lower category than their associates. Others are always happier, more famous, and more successful, worth more. Others' successes only made this person more depressed at their own status in life.

These people accept criticism as always being true. Not only do they accept criticism from others willingly, they're the ones who criticise everything they do themselves as well. The little voice in their head is always ridiculing them about their perceived failures. They punish themselves with statements such as *'I should have known that was going to happen. Where were my brains?'*

They jump to conclusions without knowing all the facts and assume they know what others are thinking. On the other hand they assume others know exactly how they're feeling as well. They should communicate with others so they can confirm their beliefs.

Indecisiveness

If you find you're constantly in a state of indecisiveness, recognise that you're not alone. Most people put off making decisions for various reasons. They doubt their ability to decide, so make *no* decision. Or they're afraid of what the result will be, so they do nothing and hope the situation will resolve itself. Recognise that some feelings of indecision are normal. It's when indecision starts making an impact on your life that you can get into trouble.

Dependency

Many children grow up feeling that they cannot think or act without first getting permission from at least one person in authority. They might be encouraged to have this self-doubt by being encouraged to rely on others, rather than to trust their own judgement. Schools instil approval-seeking behaviour where the student needs to have permission to do everything. Children who act or think independently, who rely on their own judgement, often receive the label 'trouble-maker.'

And yet, when these children become adults, we suddenly expect them to make important decisions. For some, this may be impossible. In the workforce, many employees paid to make decisions are fired, because they sit on the fence rather than act.

You cannot give your children self-confidence; they must gain it by seeing you living the same way yourself. Children learn best from the behaviour of their role models. By treating yourself like an important person [not sacrificing yourself for them] you teach them to believe in themselves. Parents should not live their lives for or through their children.

Being psychologically independent involves not needing others. The moment you need - you become a slave to others.

'People are lonely because they build walls instead of bridges'

- Dependency keeps you from feeling responsible for your actions,
- Keeps you dependent on others,
- Makes you feel you don't have to work hard,
- Makes you feel you should please others,
- Allows you to avoid guilt by doing what others expect from you,
- Makes it unnecessary to examine your wants and needs,
- Encourages you to be a follower rather than a leader.

Forgiving Others

We can allow well-meaning people to hurt us. A workmate may betray us, gossip about us or try to make us feel guilty. It's not easy to forgive this behaviour. We may feel that we're letting ourselves down, if we forgive others too easily. We wait for them to do something to mend the rift and believe they should pay for their wrongdoings. Hate may overshadow everything else in our lives. Often, forgiving is the only action that will mend and heal and can result in renewed relationships.

You may say, *'That's easy for you to say! Your workmate didn't gossip behind your back and pass on untrue information about you!'*

Here's what you can do to mend the rift. Quit any pretence that you like the person. Acknowledge to yourself that you are angry and why you're angry. Then confront the other person by stating to their face, your perception of their wrongdoing. Let it all out. Keep in mind that they're human too and they too make mistakes. Then forgive them - not just verbally but mean it. Once you forgive the person, you can get on with your life.

Many don't agree with this. They believe that forgiving wrongdoers just lets them off the hook - that it's too easy on them. In reality, your feelings of revenge tie you [the injured party] to the wrongdoer instead of allowing you to get on with your life. You should spend your energy picking up the pieces, instead of on hate and revenge.

I found that I could get on with my life when I forgave others for their wrongdoings. It's ironic that each wrongdoer in my life has been given his or her own cross to bear as payment for his or her wrongdoing to me. I just had to sit back and wait for it to happen. For instance, one boss I had was afraid that I might be after his job. He made my life a living Hell for months, which caused terrible stress and health problems for me. I finally had to admit defeat and look for work elsewhere. That man is now bouncing from one job to another, each at a lower level than the one before. He leaves behind a string of former workmates who despise him.

Inflexibility

As we become older, our ability to change with the times can be our undoing. This is especially true right now with so many technological changes happening. Unless we keep up with technology, we'll be left behind. Just think of the changes that have happened in the past three decades. Word processors replaced typewriters, FAX machines and the internet send information electronically and most clerical positions became redundant.

Managers do their own correspondence through the internet, and some can talk to their computers to produce typed messages. Very few letters are sent by 'snail mail.' People keep their daytimers in their computers and lap top computers.

Can't say 'No' to others' requests?

You're not alone if you find your self-esteem level is shaken when others ask you to do something you definitely do not want to do. Even those who have high self-esteem levels suffer from this problem. Naturally, you don't want your refusal to have a negative effect on the person, but you don't want to capitulate either.

Ask yourself whether you say '*Yes*' for any of the following reasons:

- You don't want to hurt someone's feelings?
- You don't want to explain why you want to say no?
- You don't want to say anything the other person might interpret as negative?
- You feel compelled to spend time with the person because you haven't seen him or her in months?
- The other person is particularly important to you?
- You would really like to oblige, but the timing is inappropriate.

Learning how to say '*No*' when you want to, depends on increasing:

- Your self-respect,
- Your confidence about following your standards and decisions,
- Your comfort about meeting your personal needs,
- Your comfort and confidence in pleasing yourself.
- Your understanding that you can't always please everyone.
- Your understanding that your worth does not depend on other people's judgments,

Try the following, if you have trouble saying '*No*' when you need to. Each step forward can help you learn when and how to say '*No*' comfortably.

Step 1. Pick one type of situation where you've said '*Yes*' inappropriately several times during the past few months. Concentrate on this area first.

Step 2. Identify your reasons for saying '*yes.*' Are you concerned that saying '*no*' might injure the relationship? Are you worried about the other person's feelings?

Step 3. Put together a plan of action for preventing this next time. Part of this step involves preparing yourself for such an occasion and part involves preventing the occasion from recurring.

Step 4. Practice your new response. Examine how you sound and feel, as you say *'No'* in a thoughtful way. Rehearse with an uninvolved person who has good judgment.

Note: Always know what you want before you decide to say, *'Yes.'* Don't allow yourself to feel compelled to return a favour from a friend. Stop saying *'Yes'* to people just because you believe saying no will hurt their feelings.

Fear of Success

Do you feel that if you become a success, you might lose the love and comfort of important people in your life? Do you feel you might outgrow your close friends? Do you feel that your success might force you to find new support groups and friends? If you choose to start climbing, will you feel the need to keep climbing? Maybe you're not sure how high you can or should climb before you've reached as far as you should. You'd hate to fail along the way. Some feel failing would be worse than not trying in the first place.

Others feel that they're impersonating success; that soon others will know they're impostors. They say, *'I know you think I'm successful, but I'm not.'* They don't feel that their successes are real. They feel that they got where they are, only because of good timing, connections or luck, rather than by their own talents and abilities. They suffer from anxiety and lack the self-confidence required to allow themselves to feel comfortable with their successes. They're likely to deride themselves for the small failures that come their way and concentrate more on their failings than their successes.

Some women have the definite fear that they will succeed. This is often a well hidden fear, and their actions will hamper their success. If you're a married woman, are you afraid that you might make your spouse feel uncomfortable with your success? If you're single, do you feel the number of available men willing to accept a successful female is too low for your liking? Analyse yourself to see if this is happening to you.

You'll identify this fear if the following happens:

1. You think others will see you as less feminine if you succeed. Successful females often appear more competitive than the average women. You may feel uncomfortable in this role. Many men feel intimidated by successful women and give put-downs you might have difficulty handling.

2. You may feel you have to choose between being successful in a career and having a spouse or mate. Or your fear may be that you'll lose the mate you already have. You may feel that you can have one or the other but can't have both. [Many have both.]

Anyone can overcome the fear of success if they keep in mind that they can do far more than they believe. I recommend that no one should take a promotion to a position where they know every aspect of the job. If they do, they'll be overqualified for the position. All promotional opportunities should leave room for the person to grow and learn while on the job or through additional training.

Men are never asked whether they can combine work with home life responsibilities. Men are far more comfortable with success than women, because they're expected to be successful. However, should their mate become more successful than they, life can get complicated. They're likely to react in a negative way. If men don't prepare for such an eventuality, their relationship will likely suffer.

But some men can't accept success either. For example: Martin [an accounting manager] hasn't learned how to expect success or take credit for good work. He recently found a serious accounting error that saved his company a considerable amount of money. He earned a large bonus, praise from his boss and workmates, but felt he didn't deserve the praise. Martin is unhappy and lacks any feeling of satisfaction about his accomplishments. He doesn't really believe he's a success.

Many people who fear success lack self-confidence. They often have few interests outside their work, are perfectionists and take life and themselves too seriously. A sudden success or promotion - usually brings new responsibilities and the rewards can make them feel uncomfortable. Because of this discomfort, they won't take the credit for their successes. Instead, they say it was just luck or chance. They may feel good momentarily, then remind themselves that they could have done it better, faster or more thoroughly. This leads to depression. When their next test comes along, they're certain they won't be able to succeed.

They avoid risks because they believe the fall will be so much harder on them when others discover they're a fraud. This causes a high level of anxiety. They have a constant fear of exposure that can result in stress-related illnesses such as migraine headaches and backaches.

They must learn not to compare their successes with those of others. Their aim should be to do something better than they did before [whatever it is they're doing]. They should spend more time having fun, to find activities that make them feel good and do them as often as possible.

Self-concern

Feelings of self-concern include interest, worry or anxiety. It's the cause of all the unpleasant feelings that we have when relating with others. You can probably recall an experience that caused you to feel upset and unsure of yourself. You'll find that self-concern was probably at the root of your feelings.

We all try to make a good impression on others. This is natural. Not all feelings of self-concern are bad. We tell others what kind of person we are by our ambition, regard for personal appearance, work ethic and our sense of values. This is constructive self-concern or self-love. Self-love means you love yourself: it doesn't demand the love of others.

Those with little self-love behave in self-defeating ways. They show destructive self-concern by tendencies of selfishness, fear, doubt, getting your way at all costs and have a reluctance to change. They avoid rejection by not letting others know how they really feel. Or they may encourage pity from others with a 'poor me' attitude. Some blame others for their own misery. Some act dependent and expect others to decide for them.

On the other hand, when everything goes right, they worry that things are too good. They wait for disaster to hit, instead of enjoying life. These feelings won't lead to worthwhile accomplishments or relationships with others.

Other destructive traits are jealousy or envy. If we look behind most jealousy, we'll see that it's a put-down to the person who's responding that way. They fail to understand that it's possible that others might choose another person for a mate, without it being a negative reflection on them. If a significant other doesn't choose them, it shouldn't have an effect their self-worth or value.

A rule of thumb is to stop worrying about what others think of you. How you see yourself, is the issue here. Please yourself, remembering not to infringe on the rights of others. This is not easy to accomplish. Mental control and practice over your emotions are necessary.

Women in particular, have problems doing this, because they are normally the nurturers in society and are accustomed to putting others' interests first. They need to learn to put their interests first more often simply because if they're happy - it reflects on others. This ability makes them more effective in dealing with life's problems. They learn that they don't have to rely on others to have a good day. This allows them to become more self-reliant, take responsibility for their actions and moods and make decisions for themselves.

Don't always strive to get other's approval. Make approval-seeking a desire, not a need for self-worth. The need for approval of others is based on the assumption that you don't trust yourself - that you'd better check it out with someone else first.

Can people increase their self-confidence level or become stronger mentally? Or are they doomed to go through life with the same self-confidence they have now? The answers are: Yes and no depending on their expectations.

Setting Expectations

Are you setting expectations for yourself that are irrational? Here are some fallacies you may believe are true:

- ✓ What happened in the past has a direct influence on the present, must always be remembered and will affect the future.
- ✓ When events go wrong it's a calamity.
- ✓ It's easier to make excuses than face reality and consequences.
- ✓ Everyone must love you.
- ✓ You must be completely competent in everything you do.
- ✓ You should be dependent on others and have someone stronger to rely on.
- ✓ There is only one right way to do things.

- ✓ You're bad [no matter how unimportant the event is] therefore deserve punishment.
- ✓ You have no control over outside circumstances - good or bad events that happen in life are due to chance or luck.
- ✓ There are many dangerous situations, so you have a right to feel afraid most of the time.
- ✓ You should be very upset about other's problems and must become involved in helping them solve those problems.

I'm sure you have the above feelings from time to time, but if they overshadow what happens in your life, it's time to examine your feelings. These are all irrational beliefs and should not overshadow rational thinking.

Do you do the following?

- Continually feed yourself information that perpetrates the view that your self-worth is less than others? *'I did it again! Won't I ever learn?'*
- Try to gain sympathy by making self-demeaning statements? *'What a stupid thing I just did!'*
- Bring suffering on yourself? Do you say, *'I'm not good at this,'* in the hope that others won't find fault [because you've already done so yourself]?
- Turn your anger on yourself insisting that others are better than you?

How come everyone doesn't do this? What do others know or have that you don't? It's likely that they have a better self-image that they've increased little by little. You can do the same. They don't blame others for everything that happens to them and are aware that situations ***do*** go wrong. They know the events that do go wrong, often have nothing to do with them. They quit brooding about life and make events happen.

You may be setting yourself up for failure, just by your attitude. Ask yourself if:

a) You feel you must consistently prove yourself?
b) You have a hard time dealing with emotional situations?
c) You make mistakes so you get angry with yourself and quit trying?
d) You can't be best at something, so you lose interest in it?
e) You wait, thinking situations will resolve themselves?
f) You avoid arguments by withholding your opinion?

g) You're afraid of offending others by saying what you really feel when asked your opinion.
h) Others misinterpret most of your intentions.
i) You find yourself envious of most people.
j) You resist looking inside yourself to find the 'real you?'

If any of these feelings fit you, take a long, hard look at your perceptions and work towards raising your self-esteem level.

CHAPTER TWO

HOW TO OVERCOME NEGATIVE TAPES

How do we get negative tapes?

As children we depended on our caregivers to either make us feel good or bad about ourselves. Most parents and caregivers show their love and want everything to go well for their children. Unfortunately, some don't realise that the words they speak can have a life-long effect on their children's vulnerable psyches. They probably don't realise what destructive criticism can do to the fragile ego of a child. People hear and perceive exactly what they want to hear, based on their earlier experiences, values and biases.

Parents or teachers often use such expressions as:

- *'You're not as smart as your brother are you?'*
- *'Can't you do anything right?'*
- *'What a klutz you are, that's three times you've done that wrong.'*
- *'You're the pretty one/athletic one/funny one.'*
- *'How dumb/stupid can you be?'*
- *'You ought to know better.'*
- *'Sometimes I wish I'd never had kids.'*
- *'You're a naughty girl.'*
- *'Why can't you be more like ...'*
- *'Why don't you act your age?'*
- *'You're so inconsiderate!'*
- *'Leave me alone.'*
- *'Must you always look like such a slob?'*
- *'What a spoilt brat you are!'*
- *'Shut up!'*
- *'Jenny, you're so sloppy I don't know what I'm going to do with you.'*
- *'Jackie, you're a bad boy.'*
- *'Do it - or else.'*
- *'Mary, this is a D. How dumb can you be?'*
- *'If you don't come with me right now, I'll leave without you.'*

These messages are put-downs and are almost impossible for the child to assimilate because they're coming from a person in a position of power. This puts them on the defensive and gives them negative feelings about themselves. Most of these comments label the child and give them guilt feelings for not being what the powerful adults what them to be.

Harmful negative labelling

Labels are very destructive. For instance, how can Jackie 'unbad' himself? Because the parent hasn't defined the specific behaviour, he's using that offended them, Jimmy really doesn't know where to start improving himself.

Jimmy's parents have put negative tapes in his head that may stay there until he's mature enough to realise the tapes are no longer true. But - look at the damage it has done to Jimmy in the meantime!

Do you have any negative tapes that are still buzzing around in your brain? Were you told you were dumb, so you became a school dropout? Do you still feel you're dumb, having allowed these terrible tapes to influence your ability to succeed? Did you give new activities a half-hearted try, then use the excuse, *'Well it's just because I'm dumb that I didn't do well?'* We can set ourselves up to fail with this kind of attitude.

How to remove negative tapes

Write down situations you feel you'd like to change. Are you too shy, lazy, have a bad temper, are a poor speller, have a bad memory, etc. Learn to reprimand yourself with such thoughts as:

- ✓ *'Until now I've chosen to be shy. Today I'm going out of my way to socialise with new people.'* Or,
- ✓ *'I've allowed myself to be lazy. From now on I'm going to make TO DO lists and I'm going to follow them.'* Or,
- ✓ *Today I'm going to really listen and try to understand others' points of view.'* Or,
- ✓ *'I've allowed my bad temper to alienate others. From today onward I'm going to learn communication skills to overcome that tendency.'* Or,
- ✓ *'I've always told myself that I have a bad memory, but today, I'm going to change that. I'm going to hone my listening skills and pay close attention to what people say. I'll really try to absorb important information I read and pay attention when

introduced to new people. Then I'll repeat their name mentally several times to lock it in.'

For some, it's safer to hang onto a learned response, even if it's self-destructive. To overcome such destructive behaviour the person must constantly identify positive qualities about themselves and give themselves the recognition. As well, they need to stop themselves when their self-talk concentrates only on their faults.

I had a negative tape that roamed around my brain for all my childhood years and a large portion of my adult life. My negative tape revolved around my brother Jim [who was fifteen months older than me.] He was always one year ahead of me in school. My brother was an A student with averages in the high 90s. He was not the nerdy, studious type either. He seldom cracked the books, but consistently got 90 per cent or higher in his exams.

The next year I would have the same teachers he had and got very tired of their comments, *'You're not as smart as your brother, are you?'* Instead of making me quit trying, I have to admit that I went from an average student to one who got 80 per cent in most of my tests. Inside though, I always felt I wasn't very smart and couldn't remember items like he could. [Another major mistake I made was that I compared my successes against his.]

What changed my mind about my abilities was when I realised that my brother had been born with a rare talent. He had a photographic memory [which accounts for why he didn't have to study for exams.] Once I realised this, my belief that I had a poor memory, changed drastically. I spoke to a close friend of mine about this revelation, and she snorted at the idea that I had a poor memory. *'Look at the amount of information you have to bring up from memory when you're conducting your seminars! If you had a poor memory, you couldn't do that!'* Voila - I now know that I don't have a poor memory!

Do this search of your psyche. You may find some negative tapes lurking there that should be thrown out. This will enable you to try new things with an open mind. Start small and build on your successes.

I cover how to deal with negative tapes in one of my seminars. I noticed that one of my participants was writing madly with a wide grin on his face after I had described how destructive negative tapes could be. He was a well-dressed man about thirty-five years of age who appeared to 'have his act together.' He asked to speak to me after my class and related his story to me.

When he was thirteen, he went through the growth spurt many adolescent boys do, but he overdid it and grew six inches in six months. This of course made him one awkward teenager. He could have survived this, except that his family, his friends, his peers at school, his teachers and even his gym instructor kept labelling him. They described him as clumsy, awkward, uncoordinated, bumbling and lacking in dexterity. He heard these statements so often that even he began to believe the labels.

When he was fifteen, he was six foot three inches tall, a perfect candidate for basketball. But - did he try basketball? No, because he believed he was clutzy, awkward ...

When it came time to learn how to dance with a girl, did he try? No, because he was clumsy, awkward ... When he tried to fix cars, did he succeed? No, because in his mind he was clumsy, awkward, etc.

At the seminar, he'd been busy writing down all the things he was going to try. As he said, *'I've wasted 22 years of my life thinking I couldn't do things without even trying them. It's time for me to try them all. The first activity on my list is to try basketball!'*

'The key to happiness is having dreams.

The key to success is making dreams come true.'

Constructive criticism

Just think of all the years he wasted because others had given him destructive criticism when he was a child. Constructive criticism talks about a person's behaviour; it doesn't label them. For instance [using the above destructive criticism examples]:

- ✓ *'You really excel at sports. Could you try a little harder to get better grades?'*
- ✓ *'I know you can do better than this. Look at how well you did on your last test.'*

- ✓ *'You look as if you're having trouble with this project. Is there anything I can do to help you?'*
- ✓ *'Jim, you're far too old to be pulling stunts like that.'*
- ✓ *'Jill, writing on the wall is naughty. Don't do it again.'*
- ✓ *'Bill, I've just cleaned the house. Please pick up your belongings and put them away.'*
- ✓ *'We don't allow that kind of behaviour. Please apologise to Gerry for not sharing the toys.'*
- ✓ *'Jenny, please try to be more careful with your water colour paints. They leave stains when you spill them.'*
- ✓ *'Jackie, we can't tolerate that kind of behaviour. You're not to throw anything in the house.'*
- ✓ *'Let's talk about your report card Mary. I'm concerned about the 'D' you got in math. Let's see what you can do to improve your marks on your next report card.'*

Unfortunately, parents say things in the heat of the moment little realising that their negative tapes can be 'locked-in' for part or all of their child's life. If you find you do this automatically with your child, try the following:

1. Don't speak on impulse. Walk away for a minute or take yourself away mentally for a moment, thinking of something other than the situation you're facing. Then, count to ten.
2. Develop responses to familiar problems and strive to use them. If the child balks, consider giving firm consequences should s/he not do what you ask him/her to do and make sure you follow-through.
3. Concentrate on your child's positive behaviour. Most children want to please, but if the only way they perceive they can get your attention is to be bad - that's what you'll get from them.
4. Try giving them isolation for bad behaviour or remove privileges, rather than yelling or hitting them.
5. Use humour whenever possible such as thinking of tossing an imaginary pie in your child's face if s/he did something that made you angry. This defuses your anger and keeps you more objective when dealing with the behaviour.
6. Don't say or do anything you'll regret. Think of when a child tripped and broke something. Yelling at the child for breaking the item is double punishment if s/he hurt him or herself when s/he fell.

If you were the recipient of destructive criticism, you no longer have to believe that your old tapes are correct. Could a negative tape be the reason you aren't good at that activity? If you find yourself responding badly to criticism, did it talk about your behaviour or did it label you? If the person labelled you, ask them for the exact behaviour you used to cause the criticism.

For example, your supervisor is conducting your performance appraisal. She makes the comment that she doesn't like your attitude. This doesn't enlighten you about what you did that she felt was incorrect, nor does it give any indication how you could change. If you are faced with a comment like that, reply, *'What is it about my attitude that you don't like?'*

'Well, you were rude to Mrs. Jones.' [Another label - rude.]

Be persistent and say, *'What was it that I said to Mrs. Jones that you thought was rude?'*

Only after you've been able to funnel the conversation, will you be able to find out what you did wrong and what you're expected to do in the future.

If you're a parent, catch yourself if you find yourself giving your children or others labels or negative tapes. Apologise and say, *'I didn't mean what I said and I'm sorry I said what I did. What I meant to say was ...'* and you would outline the behaviour that upset you.

CHAPTER THREE

WHERE DO YOU WANT TO GO?

'Enjoy life; this is not a rehearsal.'

Where Do You Want to Go?

To take command of your future, you have to know where you want to go, not only in your career but in your whole life. What do you really wish you were doing right now? What would be your dream job? These are usually obtainable, if you're willing to work hard and set some concrete goals for yourself.

Stop demanding perfection from yourself. Set goals you can and want to achieve. You're okay. Reward, comfort and love yourself. Recognise when others' opinions affect you or when they try to give you feelings of inadequacy or guilt feelings. Learn to cope more and defend less. Use positive affirmations daily such as, *'I am ... I can ... I will ...'* Dreams can become a reality with goal setting

'A goal is a dream with a time frame'

It's an effective method of planning for the future and gives life direction with a destination. It's important to write down your goals, so you can refer to them and can tell when you've reached them. Unless you participate in goal setting, you'll miss out on one of life's great 'highs.'

I had the opportunity of offering my goal-setting seminar in Johannesburg, South Africa in May 1993. At the end of my session, I asked the audience [black women in executive secretarial positions] to write down their 'dreams.' They were also to identify obstacles they saw in their way of achieving their goal and what steps they could take to get where they wanted to go. I then offered them a microphone so they could explain to the rest of the audience [350 participants] about their plans.

Their thoughts and dreams were similar to those found in women in first world countries, but I soon realised that they had many additional obstacles to overcome. At that time [before Apartheid was over] they had not achieved the status of being classified as 'persons,' therefore they were 'owned' by their husbands. They could not vote nor own property. Their dreams counted on the government's promise that black people in South Africa could vote [which was anticipated to happen within a year.] Some of their dreams centred on having their own businesses. I applauded their courage and felt humbled and awed by their faith in humanity. When I returned to Africa in 1996, I contacted some of these women and found that most had achieved their goals, by channelling their energies in the right direction - they made their dreams happen.

In some ways, I could relate to their hopes and dreams. I too, had been in a situation where I didn't feel I had a chance of getting what I wanted out of life. After fifteen years at home with my three children, I was suddenly forced to re-enter the workforce. I had no recent employment history, a grade twelve education and three children to support. I didn't know how I would support myself, let alone three children!

I was lucky though, because I received excellent career counselling. The counsellor encouraged me to set some specific goals for myself. The two specific goals I set were: To become the Human Resources Manager of a medium to large company. My back-up goal was to have my own business. The first goal, I expected to reach within fifteen years: the second in twenty years.

I was encouraged to cut my two major goals down into smaller goals such as:

- What kind of education would I need?
- Who would take care of my children?
- How could I afford training?
- What kind of company should I work for?

Once I had set specific sequential written goals, a strange thing happened. Because I knew exactly where I wanted to go and how I intended to get there, I reached my goals long before I expected to! I had underestimated my abilities [as most people do]. Within six years of setting my goal, [nine years ahead of schedule] I became Human Resources Manager of not one, but a group of twelve construction companies. Eight years after setting my back-up goal, [twelve years ahead of schedule] I opened my international training firm, Cava Management Consulting Services in Edmonton, Alberta, Canada.

It's been uphill ever since. I have offered seminars in Canada, United States [I opened a branch office in Maui, Hawaii)] Australia [my head office is now in Queensland] New Zealand, Great Britain, Germany, South Africa, United Arab Emirates, Bahrain, Malaysia, Indonesia, Thailand, the Philippines, Hong Kong and Singapore. I also marketed the services of twelve other seminar leaders. I have written two international best-selling books and twenty-two others that are available in paperback, eBook and audio formats.

My point is: I had dreams and made them happen. I didn't wait for someone else to do it for me. So can you. Start by setting realistic, written goals.

It's unusual how some people spend their goal setting energies only on pleasurable activities. For instance, they'll save for years for a trip to the Mediterranean - yet won't spend one minute finding out what job would be best for them. This doesn't make much sense considering that they'll be spending approximately ten hours a day, five days a week either getting ready for, travelling to or working.

Women often fail, by not setting any goals at all. Some let their parents make early decisions for them and when they marry, their husbands take over. They're ill equipped to make serious decisions when their decision-makers are not in the picture. Both women and men should leave the nest and live on their own to prove to themselves that they're capable of making their own selections and decisions before settling into marriage.

Unless you participate in personal goal setting, you'll be missing out on one of the great highs in life. Both men and women in marriage should have individual as well as family-related goals. Mainly, we set goals to better ourselves or to reach a higher station in life. Many people set goals too low or give themselves escape clauses and wonder why they accomplish so little.

We can change all this by setting concrete goals for ourselves and writing them down. Goals are statements of measurable results we want to achieve. They provide a means for translating wishes into reality. They help people know when they've achieved and provide a basis for determining where to concentrate their effort in the future.

How often should you set goals? As often as necessary. Goal setting, be it career or life, is an ongoing activity. As we set one goal, it's necessary to have another simmering on the 'back burner' that we can sink our teeth into as soon as we reach our earlier goal. Why are back-up goals necessary? If you don't set back-up goals, you'll likely find that you have a 'downer' when you reach your original goal. This happens because you don't have a back-up goal to offset the exhilaration and decline of feelings that often accompany the achieving of goals.

Think about the last time you made plans for a special holiday. Remember the plans you made and how it became a large part of your life until it happened? Do you remember too, that when you came back you felt empty somehow? This empty feeling would not have occurred if you'd prepared by having something exciting to return to. You could have planned a party with your friends to share the photographs you took on your vacation or before you went on your trip you started working towards other goals.

I found that when I reached the two specific goals I'd set for myself, I became lethargic until I got busy and set more goals for myself. I now do this is once or twice every year. I don't do this on New Year's Eve as others might, but whenever I'm close to meeting one of my earlier goals.

Should you only work on one goal at a time? No - you can work towards several at one time, possibly one in each quadrant of your life - personal, family and career.

Positive/Negative Goals

It's important that your goals are positive rather than negative. It's easier to start doing something, than to stop doing something you don't want to do. For instance, a positive goal could be: *'I'll budget my income better so that I can use it to ...'* Rather than a negative goal: *'I'll stop wasting money on unnecessary expenses.'*

Goal Clarity

Goal setters must be clear about what they really want out of life. There are four quadrants that all of us are likely to find ourselves occasionally, depending on time, interest, physical and mental health and other pressures. These are:

Goal Clarity's Low - Motivation's Low as well:

'I don't want to go anywhere, and I don't care.'

Goal Clarity's Low - Motivation is High:

'I want to go somewhere, but I'm not sure where. I'm spinning my wheels.'

Goal Clarity's High - Motivation is Low:

'I know where I'm supposed to go, but I don't want to go there, or I don't care if I get there.'

Goal Clarity's High - Motivation is High as well:

'I know where I want to go, and I want to go there.'

Of course, the ideal quadrant is where both goal clarity and motivation are high, and this takes considerable planning and soul searching to achieve. It also calls for a bit of selfishness. If you've always been trying to please everyone else all your life, don't let guilt feelings push their way forward. Remind yourself that if you aren't happy doing what you're doing, it reflects on everyone around you - your workmates, your family and your friends. So, get cracking and start setting goals for yourself.

Life Inventory

To find out where you want to go, you have to know where you are now and what your desires are. To help with this, complete the following on a piece of paper. List those things that come to your mind; don't censor anything.

1. Peak experiences I've had:

These are special moments in your life. They don't have to be the most exquisite moments you've ever had. There are or have been particular times when you felt you were really living and enjoying life to the fullest [self-actualisation.] This should be a list of situations that matter to you, because they make you feel glad that you're alive.

2. Things I do well:

This allows you to boast about yourself and focus on your strengths. Some activities you do well will be activities that are very meaningful to you. Others may bore you to death. List all that you can think of quickly. You might ask a close friend or relative to help you with this one.

3. Things I do poorly:

These are activities that you do not do well, but for some reason you want to or have to do them. You also might ask a friend or relative to help you with this one. However, don't list activities that you have no interest in doing or don't need to do.

4. Things I'd like to stop doing:

All of us have habits we want to stop. There might be things that for some reason you have to do, but don't want to do. Friends, family and close associates also may suggest some things they think you should stop doing. For example, smoking, overeating or drinking.

5. Things I'd like to learn to do well:

These are activities you must do well or activities you want to do well. We have a better chance of succeeding if we stay on the periphery of the activities that we know we do well. For example, for many years I trained in competitive swimming. Later I taught swimming, then joined the Masters' Swim Club [mature competitive swimmers] and then became a certified underwater SCUBA diver. These all have the same theme - they involve something I excel at - swimming.

6. Peak experiences I'd like to have:

These are situations you want to happen to you. Also list here peak experiences you'd like to have again.

7. Things I'd like to start doing now!

Be creative - dream a little!

8. What do you want to change or improve in your life?

a) Do you wish you had a better education?
b) What new position would you like to have?
c) What professional or occupational skill would you like to strengthen?
d) What specific improvements in your physical condition would you like to make?
e) What new activity would you like to begin?
f) What debts would you like to pay off?
g) What specific habit would you like to develop or stop doing?
h) What personality trait would you like to develop?
i) What new honour or achievement would you like to attain?
j) How much money would you like to earn?
k) How much money would you like to save each pay period?
l) Others [from personal needs above].

Life/Work

Do you wish to set goals to change any of the following?

Do you:

- ✓ Have problems with your boss?
- ✓ Feel bored with your job?
- ✓ Have trouble interacting with workmates?
- ✓ Find your workmates uninteresting?
- ✓ Feel little sense of accomplishment?
- ✓ See little chance for advancement?
- ✓ Feel the need to make a significant mark in life?
- ✓ Find you don't have enough challenges, excitement, and risk in your life?

Relationships

Do you:

- ✓ Find you don't know enough people?
- ✓ Have problems with your children?
- ✓ Find you have too few close friends?
- ✓ Need a better support group?
- ✓ Face unresolved problems with partner?
- ✓ Need more fun time in your life?
- ✓ Find that others are too dependent on you?

Individual

Do you:

- ✓ Want more money and financial security?
- ✓ Wish you had less chaos in your life – more serenity and peace of mind?
- ✓ Feel you're physically out of shape?
- ✓ Find that you don't eat properly - are over- or underweight?
- ✓ Feel you need a better spiritual life?

Using your Potential

For a completely balanced life, people must have a good mix of the following to achieve their full potential. Problems in any of the following groups can add to dissatisfaction in life:

Physical potential: They have problems with self-image, such as not being physically fit, are overweight or want to stop smoking.

Emotional potential: They suffer from too many highs and lows or have become negative thinkers.

Socialising potential: They have problems interacting with others possibly because of extremely introverted or extroverted personalities.

Intellectual potential: They're in dead-ended jobs, find they're not using their abilities, are overlooked for promotions or are under-qualified for their positions. Not allowed to use all their talents and abilities [some may find they're better qualified than their bosses.] Many have to back-pedal, so they don't step on the toes of their superiors.

Creative potential: They're not allowed to use their creative abilities - are expected to 'blend in.' Most of them use only 5 to 20% of their full creative abilities. This can start from their childhood when they're expected to blend in with the crowd [become a clone.] Adults need encouragement to open the doors to their creative potential.

Criteria Necessary for successful goal setting

To be successful, goals must also have the following criteria to be successful:

1. Be prepared to write down a specific goal definition [not a broad general one.] For example: I want a better job. This goal is too large and too general. Break it down into smaller, more specific components before tackling this goal. A revised goal could be: *'I will get career counselling and decide which of the top two careers I might pursue by May 1, 20___.'*

2. You must 'Own' your goal - it can't be someone else's. If you're a parent or supervisor, you do own the problem, if there are difficulties with your child's or employee's performance.

3. The person must make a personal commitment that they will spend the time, energy and effort to follow-through. A goal might be: *'I will get more education.'* As there are no quantitative and qualitative measures, nor time deadlines - you're not likely to meet this goal.

In addition to the above criteria, each of your goals must include:

Quality: [How good?]

Quantity: [How many?]

Time: [When is the deadline?]

Cost: [How much in time and money?]

An example is: *'I'll complete and obtain an above 70 mark in three courses towards a certificate in computer programming at the Computer Institute before June 17, 20___.'*

Goals could be short or long term. A short-term goal could take one day, one week or possibly up to six months to complete. They are usually part of long-term goals that can be from six months to ten years or more. Long-term goals are harder to realise, so if possible, break them down into shorter, more easily manageable goals.

Then there are tangible and intangible goals. Tangible goals are those that relate to something you can see and touch. Intangible goals relate to behaviour and attitudes and are harder to achieve than tangible goals.

Why is Planning Necessary?

Planning is thinking and doing things in an orderly, systematic manner that is then put into writing. Planning is done daily and ends guesswork and surprises. We plan by making grocery lists or tasks we'll do on the weekend. Organised people use To Do lists every day. Here are some of the things you should consider when planning an activity:

1. What's to be done? Be specific using quality, quantity and time to measure whether you have achieved your goal or not.
2. What results do we want to achieve? You can determine this by checking your specific goal statement.
3. Why should I do it? Define this to keep you motivated and to make sure it happens.
4. How is it to be done? Be specific, giving steps to each task or project.
5. Who is to do it? Choose the best and most economical person to do the task. If a task is delegated, the person must accept the responsibility and have a commitment to completing the task.
6. When is it to be done? To have meaning, we must set specific time frame to each step [when it's to begin and end] so we can measure success.
7. Where is it to be done? Sometimes finding the right place to accomplish a task is very important.

If the goal you've selected involves others, you'll need to get their participation in one or more of the following ways:

- Involvement in defining and setting the goal itself.
- Involvement in formulating the action plan.
- Consulting with them at crucial steps along the way before deciding.

If you need to involve others in your goal-setting plan, they'll be much more committed, if they have some say in setting the goals. Without that commitment, the best you can hope for is compliance from others - which usually means minimal performance.

Most of us tend to set goals that are too broad to be either meaningful or manageable. Visualising helps. Get a mental picture of tangible results that are realistic and achievable. Also remember the KISS principle - keep it simple sweetie. State short, sequential mission statements that make it clear exactly what you want to achieve.

Lifetime and Career Goals

To be completely successful, set your goals in several facets of your life. You'll want to make personal, family, social, financial, spiritual, community and career goals. Here are examples of lifetime and career goals.

Lifetime goal: By the time I reach 30 years of age, I'll marry, have two children and be employed as a professional engineer.

Career goal: Before December of this year I'll become Assistant Buyer for my firm [a short-term career goal.] Within five years I'll become Merchandising Manager for a clothing firm [a long-term goal.]

As I mentioned earlier, it's important that you channel you life in the direction you wish it to go. If you simply put your head down and do your work, you'll often lose track of what is really important in life. With our busy lifestyles, it's easy to continue doing what we've been doing and 'go with the flow.' Some people float through life without setting goals and drift into situations almost by accident. Some find themselves in a rut, but don't know how to get out of it. Others waste their talents and abilities waiting for 'something to happen.' Don't wait for something to happen - make it happen! Accomplish this with serious goal setting.

It's amazing how many people never spend time determining what they want out of life, nor how they intend to reach their goals. If you're already a goal setter, you may be ready for a reminder that goal setting is a life-time activity.

Think about the successful people you know. Did they put a lot of time, energy, effort and dedication into getting where they wanted to go? You'll probably find that they did, because success doesn't come without all of those attributes. You have to be willing to put out that kind of energy.

> *'Think highly of yourself because the world takes you*
> *at your own estimate.'*

Lifetime Goals

Now it's time to start your planning. Write down the following [be specific:]

1. What are your lifetime goals? [Consider personal, family, social, financial, spiritual and community.]
2. Then prioritise your goals 1, 2, 3, etc.
3. If you could live anywhere in the world - where would that be?
4. If you could have any kind of job or career you wanted, what would you want to do?
5. What goals do you expect to reach within two years?
   After you've written your responses down, read them aloud. Then ask yourself if you're now doing or working toward any of those important things. Are you planning to move anywhere or getting the education or researching opportunities to get your 'ideal' job?
   Most people get so caught up in their daily tasks that they lose sight of the bigger picture of life. We're only on this merry-go-round once, so why not ride your favourite-coloured horse?
6. How would you spend your life if you knew you had only 6 months left to live? [You have an inoperable aneurism but will be healthy until the last.]
7. If you found out you had 24 hours to live, what would be the 5 most important things you'd want to do?

On question 6, did you put down that you'd likely travel or spend more time with your family? That's what most people jot down here. Whatever you've identified in this question identifies what is truly important to you. If you said you'd spend more time with your family - why aren't you doing that now, instead of waiting until it's forced upon you? If you want to travel - why aren't you making plans now to make it happen? If you said you would get your life in order [wills, lists of investments, bank accounts, insurance policies etc.] why not do this anyway?

Sample Good and Bad Goals

Just stating your goals is not enough. Your goals must be clear and attainable. Here are some examples of good and bad lifetime goals:

1. **To improve my tennis game by June 1st, at a cost not to exceed $150.00.**

    For practical purposes, this may be okay since, presumably, the only one who needs to know, is the one affected. From a purely goal-setting standpoint however, this is weak. What does 'improve' mean? Is it related to serve, backhand, volley, footwork or all of these? If not identified in the goal itself, the specific results should be part of the action plan. This could be as simple as meeting the approval of your instructor or your tennis partner. One of the cost factors to consider would be the amount of time you'll be committing.

    Suggested: To win the approval of my tennis partner for my court performance by June1st with an investment of five practice hours per week and an out-of-pocket cost not to exceed $150.00.

2. **To give up smoking.**

    Obviously, you will need a target date at the very least. That may be all you need to add if you plan to do it 'cold turkey.' Otherwise, if you plan to taper down or introduce some compensating activities, your action plan becomes critical. You won't require cost factors unless you plan to enrol in a group or incur some other directly related expense. However, you could use the savings you'll derive by not buying cigarettes, as a strong incentive to quit.

Suggested: To give up smoking by September 1st. Action plan: Reduce to one pack per day by July 2nd: half a pack per day by August 1st: five cigarettes per day by August 15th: and none by September 1st.

3. To spend more time with my family, starting immediately.

This is a nice statement of intent [like a New Year's resolution] that has little likelihood of producing meaningful results. It needs to be much more specific and clearly would need agreement and commitment from the rest of the family. [In this case, time would not be a cost since time spent is the result you're looking for.]

Suggested: To spend a minimum of one weekend day per month with family-planned activities, beginning immediately, at an average out-of-pocket cost not to exceed $25.00.

4. To read a novel a month for the next 12 months, five hours a week, at a cost not to exceed $100.00.

This goal statement is okay. Set up a simple chart where you can record the novels you have read and when you completed them. You could cut the cost factor by using your public library.

5. To learn to square dance by September 1st.

Since, presumably, you will relate this to a specific course of instruction, this goal statement would be all right simply by adding the cost factors.

Suggested: To learn to square dance by September 1st, three hours per week for the next eight weeks, at a cost of $50.00.

Here are some examples of good and bad career goals:

1. To get a better job.

This goal is too large and too general. Break it down into smaller, more specific components before tackling this goal.

Suggested: To obtain career counselling and decide which two careers I might pursue by May1st, 20__.'

An additional goal could be:

Suggested: To speak to at least three mid-management people in marketing to find out what they like and dislike about their jobs and how they reached the level of position they're in now. I will complete this by May 15th.

2. To make sure I get to work on time starting tomorrow.

This is not specific enough.

Suggested: By May 1, 20__, I'll make sure I get to work by 8:15. I'll accomplish this by setting my alarm fifteen minutes earlier, making sure the clothes I'll wear in the morning are all laid out for easy access and will make my lunch the night before. Also I'll see if Jim can drop Debbie at the day care centre that will make it even easier for me to be on time.

3. To get more education by the end of the year.

As there are no quantitative and qualitative measures nor time deadlines or cost - you're not likely to meet this goal. In addition to the above criteria, each of your goals must also include:

Quality: (how good)
Quantity: [how many?]
Time: [when is the deadline?]
Cost: [in time and/or money.]

Suggested: 'I will complete and obtain an above 70 mark in three courses toward a certificate in computer programming at the Computer Institute before June17, 20__ at a cost less than $400.00'

Guidelines for Setting Personal Goals

The first kind of goal-setting you may try, are those related to personal goals. Here are some guidelines that will keep you on track:

1. Your goal must belong to you and be your individual goal.

You're more likely to accomplish personal goals that you set for yourself than if you strive to achieve goals others want you to accomplish. This doesn't mean you can't accept the goals of your spouse, a friend or boss as yours. You can do this, but your motivation is going to be stronger if you take some steps beforehand. Consciously think and talk through, the advantages and disadvantages of working towards a goal before deciding to pursue it.

Remember that knowledge of who we are and what we want, are essential so we can establish goals based on our own internalised values.

2. Goals need to be clear, concrete and written.

The purpose of writing goals is to clarify and make them concrete for ourselves. Writing and revising goals also forces us to make a commitment to ourselves. Once we've written a goal, we'll have more invested in it than before. Writing helps to keep the goal in front of us and reduces the chance we'll forget it, as new problems and challenges appear. It helps integrate our goals into projects and can identify conflicting goals.

3. Start with short-range goals.

Learning involves making mistakes as well as achieving success. Start your goal setting by working on some short-range goals that are easily attainable. As you accomplish these, you'll gain more and more confidence in tackling more challenging long-range goals. Short-range goals are more likely to be within your control. Don't concern yourself if you have to revise your first statement of goals more than once. Life is not stable, and situations do change.

4. Consider legality, morality and ethics in your goals.

Most people's value systems include some degree of concern with the legality, morality and ethics of their actions. You should consider these before you commit yourself to a goal. [This would include such situations as cheating on an exam or misleading others in a harmful way.]

5. Goals require realism and should be attainable.

Having a goal is the first step to action. However, if your goal is unrealistic or unattainable, it's not even a goal, but pure fantasy and daydreaming. The higher the goal: the stronger the motivation. However, if you don't believe accomplishment is possible - there's probably no motivation. If it feels right and makes sense to you and your respected friends - then your goal *is* possible.

6. Specific time deadlines aid in accomplishment of goals.

Assigning target dates for completing each step of a plan provides constant re-enforcement and a sense of accomplishment that helps sustain your motivation. You can and should adjust dates but make excuses authentic. Put crucial dates such as deadlines in your daytimer.

You might find it helpful to write yourself a contract, stating what you're going to do. Give it to a friend so you won't renege. Then, have a contract-burning ceremony or party when you achieve your goal. This kind of contract is especially helpful when you're trying to stop smoking or want to lose weight.

The next chapter will give you more pointers on how you can get down to serious goal-setting that will work for you.

CHAPTER FOUR

SETTING CAREER GOALS

'Don't fear pressure for pressure is what turns rough stones into diamonds.'

Guidelines for Setting Career Goals

What is a Career? The word 'career,' has a negative connotation to many people. It conjures up the image of someone totally dedicated to work, someone who always has his or her nose to the grindstone. If this image has put you off the idea of setting career goals, consider the following definitions - and think again.

A **job** is a position with specific duties and responsibilities. For example, teaching Grade 3 at Hillside Elementary School is a job.

An **occupation** is a group of similar jobs in society. It's a broad category that may or may not be specific to a particular company, government department organisation, industry or profession [teacher, engineer, accountant, personal assistant, carpenter, plumber, etc.]

A **career** includes all your work-related experience, including both paid and unpaid labour. Work-related experience includes full and part-time work, parenting and home making, volunteer and community work, hobbies and other leisure activities that may influence a person's work now or in the future. People may change jobs or even occupations, but each person has only one career.

'A job is what you do with your days

- a career is what you do with your life!'

How many years do you think the average man spends in the workforce before retirement? Did you guess 25 years? 35 years? These are both wrong. The average man now spends 45 years of his adult life in the workforce.

How many years does the average woman spend in the workforce [paid employment - not the volunteer kind] before she retires? 20 years? 25 years? No - the average woman now spends 35 years of her adult life working either full- or part-time and that figure is rising.

If you're unhappy with your career - how many more years can you expect to work at a job you hate before retirement? This leaves you with two distinct choices; stay and suffer or find something you like better. I'm sure you'll agree that the latter choice is the one you should choose. What's keeping you from making a change?

If you're 40 years of age [and feel you're too old to change] remember that you have 25 more years of productivity left in you before retirement. Why should you spend it working at a job you hate when you could be working at something you really like and want to do? Isn't it about time you made some changes?

Some workers are forced into setting career goals because they've been let go from a position [either laid off or fired.] For some, this becomes a true blessing in disguise because they're forced to look at their lives and make serious plans about where they want to go.

Goal setting takes a lot of effort and time. But it's worth it. If it takes you two years to decide where you want to go, that's okay, as long as you're steadily working towards finding the right career for you. Being successful in your chosen career does take time, energy, dedication and effort. Don't try something unless you really want to succeed at it. There's too much competition out there - people who know where they want to go and how they're going to get there.

Working at a suitable career can be tremendously stimulating. Those who enjoy their work, find that it generates its own momentum, and they genuinely feel they're realising their dreams. Often, they can't wait to get up in the morning. Mondays are great and they start the day running. With this attitude towards their work, they have a much better chance of progressing within the career they've chosen. The big question, of course, is how did they find the career that suits them so well? Most of these happy employees will have obtained career counselling.

Choosing the right career is very important, not only when you start, but later on in life as well. Many people go through the 'blahs' when they reach thirty-five or forty. They make such comments as, *'Is this all there is?'* What's happening is they've probably reached their career goals and find life very uninteresting. They haven't had another goal on the 'back burner' to kick in when they need one.

I'm a career counsellor and find that those with the mid-life career blahs often feel frustrated and depressed. As soon as they find a new channel for their abilities and talents, their outlook improves immediately.

Do you have concrete career goals? From the time they're about eleven years of age, most boys know how to answer the question: *'What are you going to be when you grow up?'* Ask the same question of most girls that age and they'll likely give you blank looks. Somehow, they don't think this is an important issue. For girls, learning to set personal career goals becomes a big challenge.

Reasons people end up in the wrong job

Why do so many people end up in the wrong type of job? Many have followed others' advice - their parents, relatives, teachers and friends.

The following shows percentages of why people go wrong with their careers:

1. They follow the advice of others, instead of their own instincts - 25%.
2. They blind themselves to what the job will really be like - 20%.
3. They assume they can live with a lower salary than they're used to - 20%.
4. They don't check out potential problems and issues during the interview - 15%.
5. They don't speak to others who are in occupations to see what is good and bad about each occupation - 10%
6. They impulsively grab the first job that comes along - 10%.

Planning a Career

There are five major steps in planning a career:

1. Obtain career counselling and identify your transferrable skills:

Many people stay in an unsatisfactory job because they simply don't know what else they'd like to do. If you find that you have trouble motivating yourself or you have little or no incentive to do a good job, you owe it to yourself and your company to change jobs. Because of the economic situation, some people say they're staying where they are. They don't want to make 'waves' in case they find themselves out of their existing job. They don't have to jeopardise their existing position. They could do their investigating and obtain career counselling after work or on the weekends. Their search should not interfere with their present work situation.

If you're having trouble deciding which career you should choose, find a Career counsellor while you're still employed. You'll likely find these through your local government or at universities and colleges. The most important thing to remember when filling out tests and forms is that you can't 'fudge' the answers. Be honest. Answer questions as situations really are, not the way you'd like to pretend they are. If you don't, you won't identify the applicable careers that use your unique talents and abilities and will end up with someone else's dream career.

A qualified career counsellor will help you decide which careers will use, not only your existing skills, but your potential skills as well. They can help you identify your transferrable skills that can be used in a myriad of occupations. Transferrable skills are those skills you can take from one occupational field into another.

For example, supervisory skills, interpersonal skills, aptitude with figures and scheduling skills are all transferrable skills. This will allow new horizons to open up for you.

One of my clients [who was working as a nursing supervisor] decided that she didn't want to work shift work any longer because she had a young family. However, she felt she couldn't work in any other occupation, so held back from receiving career counselling until her family situation became intolerable. We were able to identify her transferable skills which were:

- ✓ The ability to supervise others,
- ✓ Knowledge of scheduling,
- ✓ Highly honed interpersonal skills which enabled her to deal with all kinds of people from callous doctors to unhappy patients,
- ✓ The ability to keep meticulously detailed reports,
- ✓ The ability to remain calm in an emergency,
- ✓ Was physically fit,
- ✓ Had the ability to decide quickly.

These were talents that could be useful in many occupations. She just had to find which one she wanted to work in. One of her passions in life was ladies' fashions. After examining her transferrable skills, I advised her that if she got the necessary retail training, she'd likely have little trouble obtaining a position in a retail woman's shop. She admitted that she'd never thought of that as an alternative, because it wouldn't pay her enough.

I pointed out to her that her transferrable skills: the ability to supervise others [staff;] knowledge of scheduling [ordering stock;] highly honed interpersonal skills in dealing with all kinds of people [snarly clients and suppliers;] an ability to keep meticulously detailed reports [inventory and sales information;] an ability to remain calm in an emergency [both clients and staff;] physical fitness [stock-room gymnastics to reach stock;] an ability to decide quickly [special price for stock items] made her a good candidate. Soon, she received retail training and worked her way up to the position as manager of an international ladies fashion outlet.

2. Choose your career:

After rating your strengths, weaknesses, your likes and dislikes and making many choices, you'll likely come up with several choices of occupations. Choose two or three occupations.

Your next step is to determine if there is a market for those careers. Talk to at least two or three people in each of your chosen occupations. This is necessary because one of them may be in the wrong profession. Ask them:

- ✓ What do you like about your job?
- ✓ What do you dislike about your job?
- ✓ What is your normal day like? What tasks do you perform?
- ✓ How did you get to the position you're in [what education and experience are necessary?]
- ✓ If you could to do it over again - would you still choose that profession?

3. Training and education:

Plan where and when you'll receive the necessary training or education; what kind of company will provide the proper on-the-job training [if applicable;] what knowledge will you need before being ready for the next step up and so on.

Continuous learning is what you need for continuous challenge. You can upgrade and extend your job skills or follow shifting career interests to improve the likelihood of doing new work. You also can learn for learning's own sake. Aside from the specifics learned in formal courses, you have a more basic reason to start your self-education.

At work, the pace of change is continuously accelerating. People who want to learn, will seize opportunities. Learning, like any other skill, takes practice.

4. Decide how you'll obtain your career:

After you've made a choice of occupation, use the Goal Setting Plan [at the end of this chapter.] Don't forget to include quality, quantity, time and cost. This is where planning comes in. Don't procrastinate - do it now!

5. Find a position:

This can be through word-of-mouth or through an advertisement in the newspaper or on the internet. Some find a position through employment agencies. [In most countries, employment agencies don't charge the applicant - they charge the employer. So apply at several: it won't cost you anything for their help.] If you're applying to an advertisement, circle the verbs or action words they use. Then use those action words in your resume and covering letter. This will give you an edge over other candidates. Answer all questions asked in the advertisement. Recruiters look for similarities between your qualifications and the job requirements. But don't lie!

Every new job applied for, should have a custom-built resume.

6. Apply for the job:

Many people don't use a resume. They fill in an application form and hope it will represent them well. Unfortunately, it doesn't - so use a resume - a good one that 'sells' your unique talents and abilities. This applies to blue- and pink-collar workers as well as white-collar ones!

7. Attend an interview:

Usually, the only thing representing you before an interview is your resume. If it isn't 'up to par' you likely won't be asked to come for an interview. If they ask you to come for an interview, remember that you're there to 'sell' yourself - don't let shyness keep you from 'tooting your horn.' Know your strengths and weaknesses and be ready to discuss them with the interviewer. Have your facts clear in your mind, expect their questions and have information handy that they may need.

Know as much as you can about their company - its products and service. Make sure your physical appearance is neat and clean and that your apparel suits the position you're applying for. Never, under any circumstances, wear old jeans or cords to an interview. Blue-collar workers may wear clean jeans and cords, but if you're an office worker wear apparel one step up from the vacant position. The interviewer knows that you'll be better dressed than you would be on the job. So if you come in wearing an outfit with stains on it or needs pressing, they know you'll be wearing something even worse when you're on the job.

Remember that you only have one chance to make a first impression. Most employers decide whether they're going to hire you within the first four minutes of the interview. Your physical appearance plays a large role in that decision-making.

Mid-life career change

More and more people are making career changes in mid-life. A mid-life career change occurs when you switch from an occupation where you're well established to an entirely different one.

We choose some mid-life career changes - others are forced upon us. Making this change often involves leaving an established position to go to a junior or entry-level position, which may involve a significant loss in income. The individual may need additional training before s/he can even make the switch. Whenever possible, never leave one position without having another to go to.

Have you plateaued [in a rut]?

Are you trapped on the mid-life plateau? Is your life boring - every morning you get up and go to work and then come home? When you get home it's the same old routine - you read the paper, eat supper, do some work, watch TV and go to bed. Then you get up and go to work again.

Did work used to be exciting? Now you've gone as far as you're going to go. What are you going to do with the rest of your life? You hate the thought that it's going to be like this forever - but you don't know how to break out of your rut and are afraid.

If you're saying any of the above - you've plateaued [not going anywhere] and are likely feeling trapped. If you can accept that you're at the end of a phase, you can begin a new one.

More often than not, mid-life career changes affect others. Many are well established, with a network of relationships, commitments, responsibilities and obligations to family and work. Making a change of this kind can be difficult and complicated. Our burning desire for change can be offset by guilt feelings that we're imposing our needs on our families. Time is running out, but this may hold us back from making the necessary move. And yet, we feel it could be now or never and every day we spend at our present job is one day less that we have to do what we really want to do. So panic starts setting in.

Mixed in with the guilt, are fears and doubts about making the change; feelings of frustrations if we're not working towards the change; feelings of uncertainty about whether to stay where we are; hopes about the promise of a better life if we go. Like all change, this type of move offers opportunities for self-fulfilment, challenge, and personal satisfaction. However, change of any kind has a way of making us feel vulnerable and unsure of ourselves. It unnerves even the most self-assured people, so the support of family and friends becomes more and more important. Ask for their support during your career changes.

For many of us, work is the basis of our identity and self-esteem - which is fine, as long as we're successful. But promotions do eventually end, sometimes provoking a terrible sense of failure. Mastery of the work also may bring feelings of tedium. Dentists get tired of filling molars, teachers become bored with their students and lawyers get weary of divorce courtrooms. When this happens, there's a good chance they're feeling like the person I've just described. Although different strategies work for different people, there are courses of action that can take us all off that plateau.

Here are some:

Taking the initiative

Plateaued people often say, *'I do my job and just hope that something else will turn up.'* Those who work in large organisations are especially prone to being 'good' - waiting for the good fairy to notice them and reach out with a magic wand. However, if you wait for superiors [or fate] to create opportunities, you give others too much power over your life. It's your responsibility to say what you want. You know your competencies better than anyone. You're in a unique position to make a case for yourself, to change the design of your work, so that it's more challenging.

Think about the aspects of your work that give you intrinsic satisfaction - and enlarge on them. Then speak up and ask for a change. While you're unlikely to get everything you want, you're more likely to get something, than you are if you don't speak up.

Getting Ready for that Promotion:

Companies shouldn't promote employees simply because they've done well in their present position. They should be promoted only if they can handle a higher level of responsibility. Employees should ask themselves the following questions before considering a promotion:

Changing careers

A second career is a major throw of the dice. But for those prepared to take the risk, it may be the best choice of all. For example, Russ had been in retail trade all his life and his wife Alice was a secretary. Russ and Alice weren't aware of how repetitive their lives had become until all their children left home. Once they realised their lives had slid into comfortable boredom, they agreed to do something about it.

For several years, they thought up ideas and tried to develop plans to make them happen. Then one day, one of them mentioned having a bed-and-breakfast place. They looked at each other - bingo! For the first time, a possibility sounded and felt good. It would be work they could share, they liked people and they enjoyed entertaining.

They also realised that they'd be starting over, but it was exactly what they were looking for. Once they knew what they wanted, the rest was easy. They learned a lot in the first six months and they're still learning. They're also working fifteen hours a day and that's okay with them. Alice and Russ have moved off their plateau. While it was a little scary, mostly it was exciting, and they've have become revitalised.

Using skills in a different way

Plateaued people, who are unable to change their jobs, need to use their knowledge and skills in different ways that feel significant. One way to be productive is to be a mentor to younger people in the organisation. Being a mentor involves the challenge of being the wise teacher. Middle age is more likely to be a period of personal renaissance, especially if you encourage the creativity and growth of younger people. You'll create a new way to earn self-respect and it will challenge your abilities.

Another challenge is to become involved in your community and government. The volunteer sector can be as gratifying as your professional work, if you approach it with the same kind of commitment. Participation in the community offers opportunities to wrestle with different issues, obtain hands-on experience, be creative, exert leadership and make a visible difference. It's another place where you can use your leadership and wisdom to help others.

Am I competent in my present position?

If you're not a solid performer in your present position, were you in the wrong job? Would the new position be better suited and allow you to use your transferrable skills? Or could it be possible that you're not ready for a promotion? How well have you prepared yourself for the next step up?

Can I communicate effectively?

If you can't get along with workmates, clients and bosses, you'll likely stay where you are and not be considered for a promotion. You'll be communicating with others for the rest of your life and if this is a problem, you'll be living with a handicap forever unless you make this one of your primary goals.

Will I be supervising others?

If you've never supervised others before, make sure that you have supervisory training before you ask for a promotion. Pay for this training yourself if necessary. It will pay for itself ten times over if you receive a promotion.

Am I ready to be a supervisor?

Some people never make good supervisors. For instance, just because you're the top salesperson for your department, think twice before accepting a supervisory position. You require a whole new set of pre-requisites if you're a supervisor. Typically, sales people hate paperwork. Supervisors have to do a lot of paperwork. Sales types, love dealing with a variety of people, having challenges and meeting sales quotas.

Have I shown my employer that I'm serious about wanting to change?

Have you gone through career counselling, decided where you want to go and shown your employer that you're serious about your ambitions? Do this by registering in courses that will help you in your chosen career.

Are you a long-term investment?

Are you a job-jumper or can your company recoup money it might spend on training you? Let your employer know that you're serious about your career choice and show them you're serious [see above notation.]

Are you a good role model?

If you had your choice, would you be willing to work for someone like yourself? What faults do you have? Are you prepared to work on these faults and improve them? Do others respect you and accept your ideas as valid [or do you have to fight all the way to get your ideas accepted?] If the latter is the case, you need to work on your interpersonal skills.

Goal Setting Plan

Now it's time to teach you how to do serious goal setting. The following guideline will keep you on track and make your career and personal goals more concrete. It's very simplistic, but it works. Steps 4, 5 and 6 will keep you heading in the right direction and help you reach your goal.

Step 1: Describe the situation as it is now [what you're doing now.]
Step 2: Describe the ideal situation [what you'd like to be doing.]
Step 3: Identify the gap between 1 and 2. [This is your goal, which should fill the gap.]

Step 4: List the driving and restraining forces. [Driving forces describe the benefits you'll derive when you reach your goal. Restraining forces are the obstacles that may be in your way that may keep you from reaching your goal. What problems might you face? What are the possible spin-off problems?]

Step 5: List ways you will overcome the restraining forces. [This is where you'll brainstorm.]

Step 6: Formulate a plan of action that includes these four headings:
   Step:
   Date or Time Limit:
   People to Involve:
   Resources Required:

Step 7: Implement your plan of action

Step 8: Evaluate the success of implementing your plan.

Driving & Restraining Forces

In Step 4, it's important to identify the driving and restraining forces. These lists give a clear picture of the benefits you will have when your goal is achieved. For instance, if your goal was to lose weight, you'd read your driving force list when you feel tempted to take that piece of chocolate cake. By identifying the restraining forces, you'll be fully aware of the problems you might face. This enables you to come up with a plan of action that will help you go over, under, around or through obstacles you see being in the way.

Here's an example of how you could identify driving and restraining forces. Let's say your goal is to lose ten pounds by August 1st, 20___.

Driving Forces

- I'll look better.
- I'll be healthier.
- I can buy new clothes.
- I'll feel better.
- I'll live longer.
- I'll be in better shape physically.
- I can do more.

Restraining Forces

- I like to eat!
- My friends eat a lot too.

- I'll have to buy new clothes.
- Food and exercise plan might cost more.
- I'll have to exercise.
- I'll have to starve myself!

Rules for Brainstorming

Step 5 is important because it enables you to find ways of overcoming your restraining forces. To do this, try brainstorming to come up with unique or creative ways to eliminate your restraining forces.

Brainstorming started in the workplace and normally involves groups of people. It's a way of coming up with very unique ways of solving problems. The advantage of using brainstorming is that not only do you come up with Plan A, but Plan B and C as well. Many job-finding groups find brainstorming an invaluable tool. Whether you're brainstorming alone or in a group, for business or home life, use these guidelines:

1. Concentrate on one restraining force at a time. Encourage idea quantity. At this point, quality is not considered important. What you're seeking is as many ideas and suggestions as possible.
2. In group brainstorming, discourage critical judgment and evaluation. No one is allowed to say, *'That won't work because'* during a brainstorming session [not even you!] You're looking for ways of getting ideas; not trying to suppress them. Someone's idea [which really won't work] just might be the idea that triggers someone else to think of one that *will* work.
3. Encourage wild thinking and build on an idea. Offer any idea, no matter how questionable and encourage the group [or yourself] to build on ideas, altering, expanding and changing them. The purpose here is to get ideas, not to pass judgement on them.
4. During the actual brainstorming [which is of very short duration] there should be no side discussions. All members of the group are to concentrate their energies on coming up with additional ideas.
5. In group discussions, don't allow outside observers. Everyone in the room has to participate. Everyone should offer at least two suggestions during the session.

6. The brainstorming session itself should not last less than five minutes or more than fifteen. Shorter lengths of time don't allow enough good ideas to surface and after fifteen minutes, the greater portion of the ideas become clearly impractical.
7. One member of the group should take notes, recording the ideas as fast as they're offered. When working in groups it's a good idea to have the suggestions listed on a flip chart where everyone can see them. Previous ideas lead to further suggestions.
8. Have an idea or two in the back of your head to get the session started. This will provide a trigger to get the session moving. Once it begins, the ideas come fast and furiously.

In our example of losing weight, one of the restraining forces was that your friends and co-workers eat a lot too. Let's say you normally have coffee with your friends every morning and you've been in the habit of buying gooey cinnamon buns. If you want to lose weight, it's not going to be easy for you to resist, if you have your coffee break with them. You might have to grab an apple and walk around the block for coffee break to get through it. This way, you've removed one of the restraining forces that might have kept you from reaching your goal. In addition, you'll have had some exercise and a healthy snack. You'll need to tackle each restraining force so you can remove all possible obstacles.

Using the goal setting plan

To describe how the process works, here is an example of a goal taken through the process:

Step 1: The situation as it is now

I have no supervisory experience or training.

Step 2: The ideal situation

I need supervisory training, so I'll be prepared for a future supervisory promotion.

Step 3: The gap [or goal]

To obtain supervisory training [General goal]. I'll complete and obtain an above 70 mark in one course towards a Business Administration Certificate by March 15, 20__. [Specific goal.]

Step 4: List the Driving and Restraining forces

Driving forces: [Benefits of reaching the goal]

- I'll be ready for a promotion.
- I want to learn, am ready to learn.
- I'll earn more money.
- I'll gain more status.
- I'll use my abilities better.
- I feel I can do it.
- My employer, co-workers and family have offered their help.

Restraining forces: [Obstacles to overcome]

a) I'm not sure what courses to take.
b) It will cost money.
c) I'll have less time for my family.
d) I've forgotten how to study and will have too many family distractions.
e) I could have problems with transportation and parking.
f) It's a long-term goal; can I do it?
g) I won't have time to do everything I have to do.

Step 5: Determine ways to overcome restraining forces

The results of brainstorming in this example are:

a) I'll talk to the representatives at Smith College and Jasper University to determine what courses I should take and how much each of those choices will cost.
b) I'll talk to my employer to see if my company will help me with the cost of training.
c) I'll determine how I can eliminate all the extra activities that take me away from my family and from obtaining the training I need.
d) It will take time to re-learn the skill of studying - so I'll ask for my family's co-operation to give me uninterrupted study time.
e) I'll arrange to have the car and organise parking for the nights I'm attending classes.
f) I'll keep myself motivated by taking only one course at a time instead of worrying about all ten of them at once.
g) I'll resign from the condominium board, so I'll have more time to spend with my family and to take courses.

Step 6: Formulate a plan of action that includes these four headings:

Step: Contact college re: courses and parking
Date or Time Limit: tomorrow
People to Involve: college rep.
Resources Required: phone / rep

Step: Contact universities
Date or Time Limit: tomorrow
People to Involve: university rep
Resources Required: phone / rep

Step: Decide which course I'll take and costs
Date or Time Limit: within 2 days
People to Involve: boss / spouse
Resources Required: boss's and spouse's time

Step: Decide which course I'll take and costs
Date or Time Limit: within 2 days
People to Involve: boss
Resources Required: boss's time

Step: Talk to boss re: help with costs
Date or Time Limit: within 2 days
People to Involve: boss
Resources Required: boss's time

Step: Talk to family – ask for help around the house
Date or Time Limit: within 3 days
People to Involve: family
Resources Required: family's time

Step: Talk to spouse re: use of car
Date or Time Limit: within 3 days
People to Involve: spouse
Resources Required: his/her time

Step: Sign up for selected courses
Date or Time Limit: within 4 days
People to Involve: college / university rep.
Resources Required: rep's time

Step: Talk to family re: help in obtaining uninterrupted study time
Date or Time Limit: within 3 days
People to Involve: family

Resources Required: family's time

Step 7: Implement your plan of action

Step 8: Evaluate the success of implementing your plan.

Now it's time to put words into action.

1. Write down several short-term goals you'd like to reach. Before using the Goal Setting Guide, ask yourself the following questions:
a) Is my goal specific enough? Can I tell when I've reached it?
Is it a tangible [something you can see] or intangible goal [relating to behaviour and feelings?]
Is it a short-term goal or will it take a long time to accomplish this goal? The hardest goals to reach are those that are too general to gauge when you've achieved them, long-term or intangible goals. People often run out of steam when accomplishing long-term goals, so you'll need to persevere by cutting your goal down into short-term ones first.
2. Go through the 8 steps of the goal setting process.
3. Follow the guidelines and reach your goals.
4. Don't forget to have a back-up goal ready to take over when you're close to reaching your existing goal.

Goal setting - intensive goal setting - is hard work. It takes a lot of effort and time, but it's worth it. If it takes you two years to decide where you want to go and what you want to do - that's okay, as long as you're steadily working towards finding the right occupation and lifestyle for you. Good luck with your goal setting.

CHAPTER FIVE

HOW DO I CHANGE MY APPROACH TO LIFE?

'Live each day in the present and make it beautiful.'

Maslow's Hierarchy of Needs

There are as many situations that make people happy and contented, as there are motivators that drive them to improve the quality of their lives.

The most widely used theory for the study of motivation is Maslow's Hierarchy of Needs. He proposed that people have a complex set of needs that he arranged in order of importance. There are four basic assumptions in this hierarchy:

1. A satisfied need is not a motivator. When a need is satisfied, another need emerges to take its place, so that people are always striving to satisfy some need.
2. The need network for most people is very complex with several needs affecting the behaviour of each person at one time.
3. We must satisfy the lower-level needs, before we activate the higher- level needs. There are many more ways to satisfy higher level needs than there are for lower- level needs.

Consider the following and try to determine which level you're at now and what goals you could set to get to the next level:

Physiological Needs:

This is the need for essentials - food, water, air and shelter. People concentrate on satisfying these needs before turning to the higher order needs. When a person's very hungry, no other interests exist. At home, this would be the desire for proper housing, having enough food to feed the family and having a steady job to fulfil those needs.

If we don't satisfy these needs at work, we can see high absenteeism and turnover. Proper temperature, tolerable noise level and comfortable body position are important. We can meet these needs by providing several incentives including pleasant working conditions, more leisure time and avoidance of physical strain or discomfort. We can give employees more money to provide them with basic comforts or give them the opportunity of promotion so they can earn more money.

Security Needs:

This is a person's need for safety, stability and absence from pain, threat or illness. At home, this would include freedom from dangerous situations. Even a wealthy woman who has a swimming pool, may not feel secure because she's worried that her children could drown. A child may lack the security of knowing that their misdeeds will be punished in a reasonable way. A father may not feel that his home is secure, because there have been several break-ins in his neighbourhood. His teen-aged daughter may not feel secure about going out at night, for fear she might be harassed or raped. Her brother might feel insecure because he doesn't know how to deal with a bully at school.

Many workers express their security needs through requests for safe and stable jobs with good company benefits. If a person feels their job in a company is in jeopardy, they'll quit taking risks to complete tasks - will walk the middle line and become average to poor performers. Employers try to meet these needs by providing fringe benefits, safe working conditions and seniority protection [which can be a de-motivator for hard working people who see those with seniority not earning their promotions.]

Social Needs.

These are the need for friendship, love and sense of belonging. Non-fulfilment of these needs may affect the mental health of a person. A person moving to a new neighbourhood, a child starting a new school, a teenager starting his or her first job, all need an adjustment time to meet this need.

In the workplace, employees show this with high absenteeism, poor productivity, low job satisfaction, emotional breakdown, conflict with workmates and stress-related illnesses.

People who have personality conflicts with their bosses or workmates seldom use teamwork when completing tasks. Employers try to stop this by providing a friendly co-operative attitude, step in to help solve conflicts between workmates, provide an opportunity for social interaction between workers and encourage teamwork.

Ego Needs.

Ego needs include both personal feelings of achievement for self-worth and recognition or respect from others. There's a real danger to mental health when esteem is given by others because of celebrity or fame, rather than given for the person's competence or capacity to perform the task.

Status and promotional opportunities given by others provides recognition of their competence. The fulfilment of ego needs leads to feelings of self-worth, adequacy, and self-confidence. The inability to fulfil these needs may lead to feelings of discouragement.

In the workplace, if employers don't meet this need, the employees will simply channel their energies into other activities such as becoming a star bowler. Employers wish they would channel that energy into the workforce. Employers must provide opportunities for advancement, give recognition based on merit and include their staff during planning activities. Job assignments should allow employees to display their skills and give them status in their job titles.

Self-Actualisation.

Self-fulfilment or realisation of one's potential helps people reach their self-actualisation needs. Those who have attained this level, experience acceptance of self and others, increased problem-solving abilities, and increased spontaneity. Those who haven't, have increased detachment and a desire for privacy.

To fulfil the need to become everything that one can become requires that the individual has at some time partially fulfilled the other needs. However, self-actualisers may focus on the fulfilment of the highest need to such an extent that they make sacrifices in the fulfilment of lower-level needs.

If a company doesn't recognise and use the potential of both its high and low achievers and attempt to motivate people, their employees may simply move elsewhere to achieve their potential. Employers who provide the right atmosphere will see more innovative and creative production, an increased investment of employees in their work and allow more freedom for employees to make their own decisions.

Altruism.

This stage is the level above self-actualisation. This is where the person is not only content to see themselves self-actualised but wants others to become self-actualised as well. They become mentors - usually forget about competition and concentrate on developing the talents of others, with little or no thought of compensation.

We've all seen the hairdresser, who spends her off-time doing her friend's and relative's hair - simply because she wants to. Or the mechanic who looks after all his friends' cars on his off-time. Or the counsellor who spends much of his off-time listening to and helping others who have problems.

The ideal of course, is to be self-actualised and pass on your feelings of accomplishment, by helping others attain that level as well.

Rate your self-esteem level

High self-esteem is a basic human need that's closely tied to feelings of self-respect. Our positive or negative feelings start early in life and can depend on how our caregivers treated us. If our caregivers gave destructive criticism, we likely had feelings of worthlessness. These feelings can affect the rest of our lives if they aren't replaced with positive actions. Peer groups at school, brothers and sisters also influence the self-esteem level of the individual. Too much criticism, teasing or joking about their skills or behaviour will have their own negative impact on the psyche of vulnerable children.

Those who have a low or average self-esteem level are often uncertain about their self-worth. They like themselves either some of the time or most of the time, but occasionally criticise themselves for real or imagined failures. They tell others jokes about their behaviour or appearance. They rely on external factors, such as praise from their boss or tangible goods [possessions] to make them feel good about themselves. They're likely unhappy with themselves, feel unworthy of love or recognition and feel little happiness or sense of accomplishment for what they've done in life. They need to stop kicking themselves and act.

Few people have high self-esteem. Those who do are usually happy with what they're doing and do what they do, very well. They like who they are, set realistic goals for themselves and relate well with others. Striving for high self-esteem can help them to become happier, more loving and successful. They feel secure within themselves and therefore face reality, try to make decisions, and treat others respectfully.

Unfortunately, many people drift through life, floating with the tide. They respond to external events they believe control their lives. Many feel that life is a matter of luck or chance that they have little to say about what happens to them in life.

How to improve your self-esteem

Your mind works like a computer. It determines how you function in relation to your environment, with people and yourself. Your present life depends on how you and others [when you were a child] programmed your mind. This programming occurs through earlier conditioning given to you by your parents, teachers and peer groups. Unfortunately, that programming may have involved negative input that needs to be removed. Do your own inventory as follows:

1. Write a list of characteristics you like about yourself.
2. Write a list of activities you do well. [Read these two lists when you need a psychological boost.]
3. What are you doing to build on your good points? [i.e.: If you're an athlete, why not try another sport similar to the ones you're good at.]
4. Are you regularly using your talents? [When is the last time you participated in the activities you're good at? If it's been too long, get this effective ego booster into action.]
5. Write a list of characteristics you dislike about yourself.
6. Write a list of activities you'd like to do better. [When was the last time you tried to do these activities?] Could you have changed [possibly you're more mature] since you tried last time?
7. What are you planning to do to improve #5 and 6?

If a person has a low self-esteem level, s/he seldom achieves success. How is yours? So you can evaluate where you fit, complete the following questions. [Remember to answer as situations really are - not as you would like them to be.]

Rate your self-esteem level

Take a few minutes to complete the following:

1. Rate your self-esteem levels on a scale of 1 to 10 [10 being the highest:]
   (a) At work with
      (i) co-workers:
      (ii) bosses;
   (b) At home:
   (c) With friends and acquaintances:
   (d) Your over-all self-esteem level:
2. Explain the reasons why you feel your self-esteem levels are where they are.

If you answered question 2 by stating you had a poor education - then get yourself educated! If you say you're too old to do this, remember that the average man works forty-five years of his adult life before retirement and the average women thirty-five years. With these statistics, you can see that someone forty years of age has twenty-five more years to work in the work force. Isn't it worth spending some time getting educated so you can spend the rest of that twenty-five years doing something you like?

If you answered question 2 with the excuse that you don't have enough money to do what you want - maybe it's time to learn how to earn the extra money you need. Just working an extra two or three hours a week or selling some unnecessary item, could allow you to; take the trip you want to take; buy the car you always wanted; or send your children to college. You can obtain what you want if you're dedicated and willing to work hard enough.

Did you say your problem was that you still haven't chosen a career for yourself? Then, get career counselling. If your excuse is poor health - learn how to handle your stress level better. We can blame more than fifty per cent of illnesses on stress. Learning how to eliminate frustration, anger, worry and stress from your life can definitely help you in this area. Exercise regularly, watch your diet, get adequate rest and fresh air and take care of the package you're in.

Did you give the excuse that you had a bad childhood, with poverty, abuse or alcoholism at home was the problem? That happened to you in the past. If you're still allowing these past occurrences to affect you now, it's time to get professional help to get rid of them. What's important is what you do with your future despite what happened to you in the past. Use the past as a guideline of what you *don't* want to happen in the future. Learn from the past - don't repeat it. [More on this topic in Chapter 7.]

'You can't change the past - only the future'

Once you become and adult - you no longer have the right to blame your childhood on what you are now and what you've become. Only you have control over that part of your life! So get cracking!

How do I turn things around?

Personal Inventory

By now, you've probably decided where you are and where you'd like to be in the future. The next step is to start changing your life. You've learned that one of the major steps is to set specific goals for yourself. Another is changing your attitude towards yourself, your talents and abilities and how you react to others.

For the next ten minutes, think about yourself and your self-concept. Self-concept is a mental image of yourself that you carry about in your mind's eye. If you were to describe yourself to someone, what would you say? Here are several headings that can assist you in doing this personal inventory:

1. (a) What kind of personality do you have?
   (b) Is it different on the job? At home? With friends?
2. (a) How do others normally react to your personality?
   (b) What do your family members think about you?
   (c) How about our boss? Your workmates? Your best friends?

Many have taken credit for the following poem that was published several times in Ann Lander's column. It's entitled *'The Man in the Glass':*

> *When you get what you want in your struggle for self,*
> *And the world makes you king for a day,*
> *Just go to a mirror and look at yourself,*
> *And see what THAT man has to say.*
> *For it isn't your father or mother or wife,*
> *Whose judgement upon you must pass,*
> *The fellow whose verdict counts most in your life,*
> *Is the one staring back from the glass.*
>
> *Some people might think you're a straight-shootin' chum,*

And call you a wonderful guy,
But the man in the glass says you're only a bum,
If you can't look him straight in the eye.
He's the fellow to please, never mind all the rest,
For he's with you clear up to the end.
And you've passed your most dangerous, difficult test
If the guy in the glass is your friend.

You may fool the whole world down the pathway of years,
And get pats on the back as you pass,
But your final reward will be heartaches and tears
If you've cheated the man in the glass.

Can you face 'the person in the glass?' Are you ashamed of who you are or what you've done in the past? It's not too late to change your life. What happened in the past is the past - what's in the future rests on how you decide to spend it. If you've wronged someone, apologise. If you've cheated someone, make it right. Do whatever you need to do to make it possible to set things right.

Count your blessings

This is an old, but good example of how you can improve your self-image. When we write down the good events that happen to us and list our accomplishments, we can bring them out when we're feeling down. These lists can't help but raise our spirits. To accomplish this, write down situations that have pleased you throughout the day. To balance this, write down the items you're worried about. Try to eliminate as many of the negatives as possible and then concentrate on the positives in your life.

Make promises to yourself and keep them!

One problem some have in getting tasks done is that they procrastinate and put things off. You'll stop this problem [provided you're dedicated enough] because you've set time deadlines to your goals. Setting deadlines will help too, if you have problems with procrastination or lateness. Tell yourself that you'll have more patience next time a difficult client tests your willpower. Whatever you want to improve, make promises to yourself that you *will* keep them.

One man found that he could stop himself from yelling at people by placing a loose elastic band around his wrist. If he broke his promise and lost his temper, he whacked the elastic band. This punished his negative behaviour and encouraged him to stop doing it in the future. He found that he could keep his promises to himself easier with the device and eventually was able to reward himself for holding his temper in check [positive reinforcement.] What would work for you as a deterrent?

Keep a Journal

Write any accomplishments you've made during the day and how you felt about them. Add any confirmation of these accomplishments you may have received from others. Write down difficult or negative situations and how you felt about them. Is there anything you could do that would enable you to deal more effectively with something similar in the future?

Be good to yourself

Make a list of activities that make you feel pampered and a list of activities you like to do, that make you feel good about yourself. Then, do them regularly. This nurturing could be as simple as allowing yourself to take a long soak in the tub while you read a novel.

Catch yourself when using negative thinking

If you have problems with this, have friends and acquaintances remind you that you're using negative thinking. Whenever you catch yourself berating yourself or allowing self-criticism to sneak into your self-talk, stop yourself. Analyse whether the error, problem or mistake is really as serious as you're making it. Remind yourself that it's all right to make mistakes as long as you learn from them. Ask yourself what you learned from your mistake and then carry on with a clear conscience. This topic is covered in more detail in Chapter 5.

Be willing to change

We all must be flexible and able to change. What changes are you having trouble adjusting to? Ask yourself, *'What can go wrong if I refuse to change? What are the advantages of changing now, rather than when it's inevitable later?'* Unless you keep up, you'll stay behind.

People resist change because it's far more comfortable to leave situations and tasks as they are. Goal setters must be diligent because it's easy to be rigid and slip back to doing tasks the old way.

People go through four basic stages when they change the way they do anything:

1. Unfreezing: This happens when you unfreeze your regular way of doing activities and allows you to accept new ideas. This involves breaking down the old way you did something that can involve customs and traditions.

2. Changing: This provides a new pattern of behaviour and identifies a new way of doing something. To keep you on track, you must identify the driving and restraining forces and obstacles you'll have to overcome.

3. Unfreezing: The new idea replaces the old one and the new way is frozen, so you don't revert to the old way. This takes a considerable amount of effort, because doing it the old way is sometimes easier or more comfortable for us.

4. Commitment: The person has made a commitment to do it the new way and seldom reverts to doing things the old way. Others may try to keep you from making any drastic changes in your life. They'll find all kinds of objections about why you shouldn't do what you've decided to do. The following checklist will help you cope with objections more effectively if you anticipate you might run into resistance.

1) Pinpoint the objection. Write it down in clear and concise language.
2) Don't take the voiced objection for granted. People sometimes voice one complaint to mask another they'd prefer to conceal.
3) Anticipate and prepare for as many possible objections as you can. Develop a plan for handling each objection.
4) Consider bringing up significant objections yourself, instead of waiting for the other person to do it.
5) Work out a practical way to eliminate the objection if you possibly can.
6) If you're unable to eliminate it, try to find a way to compensate for it.
7) Rally enough benefits to win the person's support and co-operation despite the objection.

8) Collect as much irrefutable evidence as you can to convince the person you're trying to convince, that his or her objection is ill founded [if this is the case.]
9) Find a way to ease the person's mind, to make it less risky to do it your way, despite their objection.
10) Spoon-feed your idea or proposal gradually. Don't try to get immediate acceptance or compliance. His/her objection may be nothing more than a delaying tactic - the person's natural resistance to change.

Support Groups

Many adults suddenly learn that they've exchanged roles with their parents. Often those in middle years who are still responsible for growing children, find they have the responsibility for aging parents as well. Suddenly the parental support they had expected to last a lifetime and had counted on has disappeared. Some feel as if life has cheated them by this role-reversal and they feel adrift.

The sudden death of a parent may make a person think [possibly for the first time] about his or her own immortality. Strong friendship with other adults is necessary now to replace the missing parental guidance they may have counted on up to that time.

The Importance of Friendships

If you've had a bad day and need someone to share it with - who would you contact? Everyone needs others to help them through their bad days and to celebrate their good ones. The more the merrier but having two people on call is definitely better than having only one, because that person might be having a bad day as well. Even more effective are support groups that can help you deal with special problems such as alcoholism, drug, wife or child abuse, depression, or severe emotional problems.

Those who find they have few close relationships with others find that they're often lonely. Some feel abandoned. If this describes your situation, go out of your way to set up a support group that will be there to help.

Friendship requires trust between people and a degree of intimacy some may want to avoid. Your need to let people see the 'real you,' my be overshadowed by the fear that others may use that weapon against you in the future. True friendships have a level of intimacy where the individuals trust and rely on consistent behaviour from the other. Only when this trust is evident, can two people become truly close.

If you watch people getting to know each other [whether they be of the same or alternative sex] there are several steps they take before they fully trust each other:

One person reveals information that is of a personal nature. The second person accepts that trust and reveals similar information about themselves.

As the trust grows between these people, the trust enlarges, and the participants reveal more and more of how they really feel about issues. This could be almost instantaneous or could take months to occur depending on the comfort zone of the participants.

This feeling of trust could end suddenly if one person does something that the other feels is a betrayal of that trust. This does not have to be something verbal. A person might have said they'd do something and didn't follow through or they were late for a meeting or anything that could shake the trust in either participant. The person who feels betrayed must use feedback to share his/her feelings with the other.

Male friendships

Most male friendships revolve around activities. Within the past generation this has all changed. The biggest change in friendships is that men and women now have solid, long-lasting platonic friendships.

Over half of married men, identify their wives as their best friends. For some, their wives are the only ones they'll bare their souls to. If their marriage breaks up, they have the double grief - from losing their marriage and their best friend at the same time.

Men should cultivate warm trusting friendships with their male friends as well. Some will never be able to break down the stereotype that it's manly to remain the 'strong silent type.' So they bottle everything inside and refuse to accept the support of others. They find it impossible to be intimate with another male to the level where they can 'bare all.'

Men have had access to a system of friendships that have been dubbed the 'old boys' network' for centuries. They met in taverns, exclusive professional and social clubs [where they didn't allow women] and discussed business and sporting activities. Few, if any discussed any topics that had a personal nature. Men seldom worked in teams with or networked with women. However, men in the 'baby-boomer' era are less authoritarian and more team-oriented than the older generation of men in the workplace. They're learning to trust other men with their feelings and negative emotions.

Only one-third of single men [compared to three-quarters of single women] say they have a best friend. If a strong network of friends and supporters are not available, get one for your mental health's sake.

Female friendships

Back in the '60s our mothers called their best female friends, their girlfriends. After husbands and children were disbursed in the morning the girlfriends gathered at one home or another. They drank coffee, gossiped, shared recipes and secrets. They cared for and relied on one another. This stopped the minute their husbands appeared on the scene. The man of the family won out over friends.

Now, women meet some of their closest friends at work and maintain their friendships long after they've moved to different companies. Because of lack of time, when women get together, they get right down to the nitty-gritty issues. There isn't enough time for chitchat, so conversations deal with deep and meaningful topics.

Today's women meet under different circumstances - in conference rooms and restaurants. There is less time for exchanges and the topics are different. Instead of discussing recipes, they are more likely to discuss some professional crisis they're facing and the most recent fast-food ideas they can use to prepare dinner.

Factors that can have a profound effect on friendships, such as getting married, having a baby, or getting divorced are more easily overcome when strong bonds are there.

What has changed this attitude in women? Children often move far away from their childhood support groups of siblings and parents and find themselves facing problems their parents can only guess at. Problems such as how a woman can climb the corporate ladder, what she should wear to look successful, should she consider a common-law relationship, what about birth control and abortion, how to handle two-income family problems and how to balance work and home responsibilities. This is where other female friends provide the input. The experiences of the two generations have become so different in such a short time that if you really want to talk openly and make sense of life, your contacts with your contemporaries are crucial.

In many cases, women use friends as stand-ins for family. They're finding their friendships with other women to be the most intimate, profound and durable relationships in their lives. In many, these ties are stronger than their family ties. Female friendships usually focus on talking about feelings and their personal lives. Some female friendships can be stronger and longer lasting than that with their husbands.

As one woman put it, *'My friend Sally and I go way back to childhood. I can tell her anything and we share all our feelings. I'll never have that kind of intimacy with my husband because he just won't let me get close enough to really understand his true emotions. He never shares his deepest feelings with me.*

When I see he's distressed about something and ask what's wrong, he shrugs me off with, 'I don't want to talk about it.' When he does this, I feel shut out by him, but nothing I say can convince him how I feel. He accuses me of being too sensitive. I've come to the conclusion that nothing I do, will overcome the lifelong conditioning that taught him to mask the negative feelings he has. The last thing he can do is talk to me about it.'

The technique of feedback

Feedback happens when you share the feelings and reactions you're having about the behaviour of others, with those people. Positive feedback is given when someone does something that has pleased you; negative when they have done something that annoys or disappoints you. It's much better to tell someone that what s/he's doing is bothering you, than for the person to remain oblivious to your unhappiness. It also allows us to tell others how proud we are of their behaviour.

There are many different times when feedback is effective. For example, you should:

❖ Let others know when you don't understand what they've said.

- Let others know when you like something they've said or done.
- Let others know when you disagree with them.
- Let others know when you think they've changed the subject, fail to make their point or have repeated themselves.
- Let others know when you're getting irritated.
- Let others know when you feel hurt or embarrassed.

Feedback also helps you keep in touch with your reactions. It enables you to deal with situations before they turn into negative feelings of frustration, anger, hurt, defensiveness, defeat, fear, depression, dependence, weakness or defencelessness. Most women are comfortable saying they have such feelings, but we socialise men to believe it's a weakness to acknowledge them. This limits their options for expressing their feelings.

Many men respond as if they're angry [an acceptable reaction amongst men] when in reality, they may feel hurt, defenceless or afraid. Their ambiguous behaviour confuses women and widens the communication gap between men and women. This gap will close when men stop to analyse what they're really feeling before they react.

To be effective, there also must be a foundation of trust between the sender and receiver of the feedback. Otherwise, the feedback could be misinterpreted as a personal attack. The recipient may hear only critical words and react defensively rather than listening to what is said.

How to give positive feedback

Nothing makes others feel better about themselves than to have someone praise them for a job well done. This has a dual benefit if the compliment is authentic. You make them feel more comfortable around you. They'll seek your friendship so they can continue to receive the positive vibes you give them. Don't however give marshmallows that are unauthentic compliments. The recipient will know the difference and will be wary of your opinions in the future.

Praise is the best motivator of people, whether they are a family member, workmate, or friend. Unfortunately, most people hear all about their mistakes they've made, but seldom about the tasks they did correctly. Why do we concentrate so much effort on the two per cent a person did wrong, instead of the ninety-eight percent they did right? Consider this, whenever you're assessing how well someone completed a task.

Those who're given recognition for work well done will usually perform at the same level the next time, because they'll receive much more pleasure from the work they do.

How to accept compliments

Many of us have difficulty receiving compliments graciously. We discount or refuse to accept them with such comments as: *'Oh, I could have done that better,'* or, *'This outfit's as old as the hills.'*

If you don't accept compliments graciously, what are you telling the person giving you the compliment? You're implying that s/he is insincere, has poor judgment or is lying. You've repaid a person's kind words with a negative rebuttal. Remember this the next time you discount a compliment. A simple, *'Thank you.'* Or, *'It's one of my favourites.'* will suffice.

How to give negative feedback

When dealing with tasks people do wrong use tact and diplomacy and the person will likely change his or her negative behaviour.

When others do something that bothers you, it's up to you to explain to them in an effective way, just how you feel about their behaviour. Identify what they're doing that bothers you and give them an opportunity to do something about it. You're being unfair to others when you don't communicate these issues to them.

Consider the following series of events:

When a person does something that bothers you, a small blip occurs on your 'screen of annoyance.' Because it's only a small blip, you decide to say nothing. The person does something else that annoys you and another, bigger blip occurs on your 'screen of annoyance.'

These blips soon collect, and you could have a major blow-up with the person. The most trivial final incident could trigger this response. Instead, you need to handle each blip immediately instead of recording it on your 'screen of annoyance' for a later blow-up.

There are three steps in the process of feedback.

    a) Describe the problem or situation to the person causing the difficulty.

b) Define the feelings or reactions [anger, sadness, anxiety, hurt or upset] the problem or behaviour has caused you.
c) Suggest a solution or ask the person to provide one.

Here's an example:

A female friend of yours has the bad habit of interrupting you in mid-sentence. This interferes with your concentration, and you find you get upset every time she interrupts you. Your first reaction might be to blast her with a statement such as, *'Will you please stop that!'* Because she probably is not aware of how her actions are affecting you, she'll likely become defensive.

What you should say instead is, *'I know you're probably not aware of this, but when you interrupt me, I feel as if you think my comments aren't important. In the future, could you please let me finish without interruption?'*

a) Describe the problem or situation to the person causing the difficulty - the person interrupted you.
b) Define the feelings or reactions - you feel as if the person thinks your comments aren't important.
c) Suggest a solution or ask the person to provide one - you suggest that in future they let you finish without interruption.

Suppose this person interrupts you again, what should you tell her? [Remember, this might be a habit with her and she may have done it without thinking.] What would be your response be? Repeat your original comments. *'When you interrupt me, I feel as if you think my comments aren't important. In the future, could you please let me finish without interruption?'*

During your next conversation with her, guess what happens? She's at it again. What should you do now? Some would suggest that you just ignore her interruptions. Instead say, *'Twice yesterday I mentioned that when you interrupt me, I felt as if you thought my comments weren't important. Can you tell me why you're still doing this?'*

What you're doing is making her account for her aggressive actions. [Yes, she's being aggressive, because she knows she's bothering you by interrupting.) Your next step is critical. Explain what you'll do [consequences] the next time she interrupts you.

This is the step most people miss. You could say, *'If you interrupt me again in the future, I'll simply walk away from you.'* A word of caution here, you must mean what you say.

Your friend apologises and promises she won't do it again. Another day goes by and she's at it again! What should you do the fourth time? Follow through and walk away from her when she interrupts you. Don't say you'll do something if you're not ready to follow through! The consequence must match the annoying incident.

You might ask yourself, *'Will this person like me after I've walked away from her?'* Possibly not, but you'll show her that you were serious when you discussed the problem earlier. Don't let guilt step in and make you feel bad. She's the one who initiated your action of walking away from her - not you.

This approach often gets the results you're after when other approaches fail. Use this technique whenever a person's pen clicking, gum chewing, chair squeaking or loud voice affects your performance at work. Use it when people are late for appointments or when their actions keep you from doing your job correctly.

To recap the four major steps in the process of feedback:

Feedback Steps

1. Follow (a), (b) and (c) steps from process of feedback.
2. If it happens again - repeat Step 1.
3. Ask the person to explain why s/he's still doing something that s/he knows annoys you.
4. Explain the consequences should the behaviour or situation happens again.
5. Follow through with the consequences

Here are some general guidelines for giving negative feedback:

- ✓ Be sure the person can change whatever is bothering you. For example, a woman who is thirty-five years of age and bites her fingernails is not likely to stop biting them just because it bothers you. And a person with a facial tic can't stop that behaviour either.
- ✓ Make sure your complaint is worth the effort it takes to change it. Don't nitpick.
- ✓ Be sure the person receiving the feedback is ready for your criticism.
- ✓ Base your comments on facts - not emotions.

- ✓ Give feedback as soon after the event as possible.
- ✓ Pick a convenient time.
- ✓ Pick a private place.
- ✓ Concentrate only on what you can change.
- ▪ Request the receiver's co-operation.
- ✓ Focus on one item at a time.
- ✓ Try to be helpful.
- ✓ Encourage the recipient to provide feedback in return.

If you've slipped into the role of being a negative person or have to deal with negative people, the next chapter will interest you.

CHAPTER SIX

HOW CAN I BECOME A MORE POSITIVE-THINKING PERSON?

How to maintain control during negative situations

Do you have mood swings that affect the kind of day you have? Are you up one day, down the next - up one hour, down the next - up one minute, down the next? Many times, this depends on what's happening around you. Somebody snarls at you or gives you a mountainous job to do and you think, *'Oh God, give me strength!'* It's the little annoyances that can ruin your day, so if you can handle the little ones constructively, you'll be ahead of the game. My book **Dealing with Difficult People** deals extensively with this topic.

If you believe that outside circumstances cause unhappiness and that you have no control over those circumstances - you're wrong. Actually, outside forces and events [while they can be physically assaulting] usually are psychological in nature and cannot be harmful to you unless *you allow* them to affect you. You can control and change your perceptions, evaluations, and internalised feelings. Happiness comes largely from within and even if external events irritate or annoy you, you have control over how you react to them. You can disturb yourself by telling yourself how horrible it is when someone is unkind, rejecting, annoying etc. If situations cause you to feel disturbed or your emotions are in turmoil, you have given over the control of the situation to the person who stimulated your feelings.

If you allow others to dominate whether you have a good or bad day, you're relinquishing an important part of your self-esteem. This can make it difficult for you to remain a positive-thinking person. If you aren't in control of how you react when others behave badly, you owe it to yourself to learn how to do so.

My life changed when I realised that I could choose how I reacted when faced with difficult situations. I could either take the bad feelings others tried to hand me or simply not take them. When I learned this simple technique, I found I had far more control over my every-day moods. Gone were the roller coaster mood swings of the past. Other people didn't decide what kind of day I'd have - I did!

You too can have this control. Mind you, there will be exceptions to this, but most moods and reactions you can control.

Picture this scene: You're driving home from work, feeling pretty tired from a stressful day at work and find yourself fuming because there's a traffic jam AGAIN! You feel as if you spend half your life waiting in traffic to get home. You finally get home, stride through the living room [past your children] and slam your bedroom door. You've allowed the traffic jam to get you all steamed up.

And it doesn't stop there. What happened to your two children who were sitting in the living room watching TV when you strode by? They likely wondered what they did to make you so mad at them. This puts them on edge - so they snap at each other during dinner. You can see how your bad mood has a domino effect on others.

When you were driving home, you had a choice about how you'd react. You know you're likely to face traffic jams on the way home - it happens three out of five days! So why did you allow yourself to get so upset? Try leaving half an hour later. This may get you home just ten minutes later, but with far less harassment.

Could you vary your work hours to eliminate some of the negatives you receive now? If you can't arrange this, resolve that you won't allow yourself to get steamed up driving home. Buy some CDs that have calming music and listen to them enroot and allow yourself more time to get home.

Possibly your wife's hours differ from yours and you're responsible for getting dinner started. Think of alternative solutions. For instance, get your two teen-aged children involved in starting or preparing dinner. This relieves your need to rush home from work and the hassles it causes.

Another example: A client starts bawling you out, really takes a strip off you for something that wasn't your fault. Were you able to 'keep your cool,' or did you blow up and regret it?

As soon as you feel yourself getting uptight and feel the need to defend yourself - STOP. Analyse the situation - and likely as not, your company or the situation has upset the customer - not you. You just happened to be there. Therefore, there's no need for you to defend yourself. Instead, concentrate your efforts on solving the person's problem. They end up happy and so do you - a win/win situation.

The first step to keeping your cool is to change your responses to negative situations. Here's another example: You've worked hard completing an assignment and are very proud of your accomplishment. Then you wait - and wait - for recognition from your manager. Is it likely to come? In many instances - no. You're much more likely to hear about the small portion of the assignment you did wrong.

In addition to this, you're probably your own worst critic. There's a little twerp in all of us who is always criticising us. It makes such comments as, *'Well, you goofed again! Can't you do anything right?'*

Learn to stop criticising yourself and start giving yourself positive reinforcement. If you've done a good job, mentally pat yourself on the back with such thoughts as, *'I'm really proud of how I did that job.'* Don't count on others to do this. Then if they do, think of their praise as 'sugar-coating' - but you don't need sugar-coating on your desert every night, do you? The person you should be trying to please is yourself. Never compete against the record of someone else. Just improve your own record of accomplishments. Give yourself a small reward when you've accomplished something you're proud of.

Remember, you choose to:

- ✓ Get upset in traffic jams,
- ✓ Get angry at the driver who cuts you off in traffic,
- ✓ Become irritated by your customer's bad mood,
- ✓ Feel guilty when you can't meet a client's needs or when you can't understand what someone's saying on the phone,
- ✓ Become stressful when an extra batch of work is dumped on your desk or become depressed simply because it's Monday morning.

What you do after something negative happens to you is your decision. If you allow someone or something to upset you, you've made the wrong choice.

By the time you're an adult, you should be able to throw away negative information and replace it with positive information. If you do this, you'll have control over your behaviour, feelings, your inner self-confidence, and your outer personality.

'Believe that your life is worth living and

your beliefs will help create the fact.'

You and your bad mood

[Permission given by Canadian Mental Health Association]

Sometimes I feel so useless and afraid.

Sound familiar? Depression is the most common and perhaps the oldest known emotional problem. Socrates described it as melancholia. Lincoln suffered from depression most of his adult life. Churchill called it his 'black dog.' Some people say they have the blues or that they are in a bad mood. It doesn't matter what it is as long as you recognise that your bad mood is not unique.

Depression can be caused by chemical changes in the body; by the way we react to events in our lives or by events in our distant past, which we thought, we had forgotten.

We all have periods when we feel worthless, afraid, useless or alone. Often circumstances, such as the death of someone close, divorce or the loss of a job can trigger a depressed mood. This is normal, but when the depression lasts a long time or gets in the way of you being yourself, you should seek professional help. If your depression is not severe, there are ways you can help yourself.

If you have the blues, you CAN help yourself.

1. Concentrate on doing things that you do well in order to build up your self-esteem.
2. Engage in physical activity of some kind.
3. Talk your feelings over with someone you trust. And don't forget your community 'hot line' if you want to talk anonymously.
4. Focus your energy upon someone other than yourself. Visit someone who's ill or lonely.
5. Break up your usual routine. Take a different route to work. Eat something new for lunch at a different time and place than usual. Take a vacation if you can.
6. List your personal and professional accomplishments.
7. Even though you may not feel like it, work at making your physical appearance as nice as possible.

Get cracking ... there's someone out there who can help you.

If your blue mood persists and becomes something you can't handle alone, seek professional help. A family doctor or social service agency can refer you to sources of help.

Remember that depression is one of the easiest of all conditions to treat and cure. You should seek treatment when your depression is severe, just as you would seek treatment for a physical disorder.

Positive vs. Negative Thinking

Positive thinkers take the time to look at themselves objectively. They know what they do well and do what they do well, as often as possible. This gives them good feelings about themselves. They're also aware of activities they don't do well. Instead of sweeping this knowledge under the rug and ignoring it, they do something to improve the situation.

All of us have tasks we hate doing. That shouldn't mean that we allow ourselves to do a careless job. Instead, get these kinds of jobs out of the way first, so you can enjoy the rest of your day. Learn how to do these duties as well as you can and your feeling of doing a good job will increase accordingly.

Get the distasteful chores done first. Try this if you find you procrastinate and have nothing but difficult tasks left at the end of the day.

Positive vs. Negative Self-talk

Determine how you would react in the following situations:

a. A party where you don't know anyone.
   Negative: No one will want to talk to me.
   Positive: Wow. Here's my chance to meet new people.

b. A difficult test.
   Negative: I'm sure I'm going to blow it no matter how hard I try.
   Positive: I can hardly wait to get into the classroom.

c. Your first-time skiing.
   Negative: *I'm going to be such a klutz. I'll probably end up breaking an arm or a leg!*
   Positive: *After a day or two on the bunny slopes, I can do it!*

Negative Thinkers

The following describes the attitudes, behaviour and results of a Negative Thinker:

Attitude: envy
Behaviour: inconsiderate
Results: worry

Attitude: greed
Behaviour: pessimistic
Results: tension

Attitude: anger
Behaviour: cruel
Results: despondency

Attitude: conceit
Behaviour: weak
Results: frustration

Attitude: cynicism
Behaviour: cold
Results: job weariness

Attitude: self-pity
Behaviour: rude
Results: unhappiness

Attitude: suspicion
Behaviour: sour
Results: failure

Attitude: indecision
Behaviour: drab
Results: sickness

Attitude: criticism
Behaviour: irritable
Results: poverty

Attitude: inferiority
Behaviour: undetermined
Results: loneliness

Attitude: defensive
Behaviour: fatigue
Results: anxious

Attitude: fearful
Behaviour: boredom
Results: dissatisfaction

Positive thinkers:

The following describes the attitudes, behaviour and results of a Positive Thinker:

Attitude: understanding
Behaviour: enthusiastic
Results: success

Attitude: anticipation
Behaviour: decisive
Results: recognition

Attitude: expectations
Behaviour: courageous
Results: security

Attitude: confidence
Behaviour: optimistic
Results: high energy

Attitude: patience
Behaviour: cheerful
Results: achievement

Attitude: tranquillity
Behaviour: considerate
Results: happiness

Attitude: decisive
Behaviour: friendly

Attitude: sharing
Behaviour: courteous

Results: growth	Results: adventure
Attitude: belief	Attitude: warm
Behaviour: sincere	Behaviour: friendship and love
Results: good health	Results: relaxed, inner peace

Here's an example of positive thinking:

Bill had applied for a position he felt he could handle easily. Shortly after the interview [which he felt had gone well] he received a rejection letter. He concluded that the reason he hadn't received the job was because, if anything, he was overqualified for the job. He resumed applying for other suitable positions. His optimistic approach [tempered with realism] ensured that he would be successful in finding a suitable position.

Brian, on the other hand, applied for a position, received a rejection letter, and simply quit trying to get another job. He concluded, *'I'd better stay where I am. I'll probably fail if I apply for others and besides, my employer might find out and fire me!'*

Such irrational thoughts will probably keep Brian in his dead-ended position. His pessimistic approach ensures that he'll stay exactly where he is, with little chance for advancement. He's a negative thinker. Brian is likely the type of person who whines and complains about life, but seldom takes action to improve it. Whiners and complainers drain the energy from everyone around them. Others may feel used by those who are constantly seeking their attention with their complaints. It's hard for positive-thinking friends and acquaintances to be around this kind of individual and many shun them - adding to their negative feelings about themselves.

How to deal with whiners, complainers, and bellyachers

If you must deal regularly with individuals who bombarded you with complaints, you might find yourself pulling your hair out trying to stay sane when they're around. Or, are you a complainer yourself?

A friend of mine was a whiner and complainer. I got tired of hearing her beefs, yet she had many good qualities that made me want to keep her friendship. One day after I'd listened to her drone on about several complaints [the same ones I'd heard voiced many times before I decided to try to help her solve her problems. She was wasting so much of her energy just worrying about her problems that she had none left to spend on solving them. She was also wasting my time.

Here are the steps I used to help her find solutions to her problems. [If you find yourself whining and complaining, try this process on yourself:]

1. I obtained her permission to help her solve her problems.
2. I had her write down the specific problem, including all necessary details. It was important that she wrote it down so that the problems became more real. It also helped her to focus on defining the specific problem she was trying to solve. We tackled only one issue at a time.
3. I asked her to write down all the possible solutions to the problem. At this stage I could suggest other alternatives. [If you're working through your own problem, you might consider asking a friend to help you through this stage of the process.]
4. Under each solution, I had her write the pros and cons [advantages and disadvantages] of each solution. It might be a good idea to use a point system that identifies important factors. I encouraged her to be unemotional - to pretend that it was someone else's problem she was solving.
5. I asked **her** to choose the best solution. This is the stage where she asked me, *'What do you think I should do?'* I didn't take the bait. If I told her what I thought she should do and the solution didn't work, I might have set myself up for her to reply, *'I told you it wouldn't work!'* Complainers are prone to passing the buck when making decisions. On the other hand, if you **are** an expert in that particular area - you could give her your professional opinion.
6. I had her set up a plan of action to make the solution happen.
7. Later when she was still whining and complaining about the problem we had worked on – I refused to talk about the issue again.

If you're counselling others and helping them through problem solving, use the above steps to help them come to a conclusion. After step six, they're on their own. If they complain to you again about the problem say, *'You know exactly what you have to do to solve this problem. I don't want to hear another word about this until you follow-through with your plans.'*

If they refuse to let you help them [step 1] go immediately to step 7 *'If you won't let me help you solve this problem – I don't want to hear about it again.'* This stops whiners and complainers from ruining your day and pressing their negative thinking on you.

Are you a positive/negative thinker?

To determine how positive you are, answer these 15 questions as honestly as possible. To score yourself, use the scale listed below:

Always or Almost Always- 4
Usually- 3
Sometime- 2
Rarely- 1
Never- 0

1. Are you a happy person?
2. Are you surprised when a friend lets you down?
3. Do you believe the human race will survive past the 21st century?
4. When you think back over the past few months, do you remember your little successes before your failures and setbacks?
5. If you made a list of your 10 favourite people, would you be on it? [Do you like your own company?]
6. Do you believe that, overall, your state of mind has had a positive effect on your physical health?
7. Do you feel comfortable making yourself the butt of your own jokes?
8. Are you quick to spot the hidden advantages when the unexpected, forces you to change your plans?
9. When you catch a stranger staring at you, do you conclude it's because s/he finds you attractive?
10. Do you like most of the people you meet?
11. When you think about next year, do you think you'll be better off then, than you are now?
12. Do you often stop to admire items of beauty or interest?
13. When someone finds fault with you for something you've done, can you tell the difference between useful [positive] criticism and 'griping' [negative] that is better ignored?
14. Do you praise your spouse, best friend or lover more often than you criticise him or her?

Your score:

49 to 60: Excellent. You're a genuine positive thinker.
44 to 48: Good. You're a positive thinker ... usually.
39 to 43: Fair. Your positive and negative sides are about evenly matched.
38 and below: Needs Improvement Negative pattern showing. Where could you improve?

Signs of Having a Negative Attitude

In relationships, a negative attitude is as harmful as alcoholism or drug abuse.

Ask yourself if you have ever:

- Refused to accept a new job because you're afraid you might not be up to the challenge?
- Withdraw from a relationship with someone of the opposite sex because you believe the person was more attractive, smart or worldly-wise than you are?
- Hesitated to try new activities because you didn't want to fail or look like a loser to others?

If so, you're allowing negative-thinking to interfere, with your ability to try new activities. Many people with low self-esteem are negative-thinking addicts. They concentrate on what they can't do, rather than on what they can do.

Many come from dysfunctional homes that lack a healthy, supportive atmosphere or are missing the help from other support groups. These people constantly compare themselves with the accomplishments of others, rather than their own level of accomplishments. They may have been reminded as children that they weren't as good as a sibling, friend or relative. These people focus most of their attention on their failures, not their successes and have difficulty accepting authentic compliments.

Is it possible that you're spending too much time with negative-thinking people? If so, you may have to stop associating with some of them. I've learned to weed out some of my negative-thinking friends and encourage you to do the same. This includes relatives that can ruin your day. You can't eliminate them entirely of course, but you can limit the time you spend with them.

Eliminate the negative aspects of your attitudes and behaviour and you can't help but improve your approach to life. This will enable you to become a more positive thinker or help you to stay one. If you deal with negative clients daily, it's essential for you to find a balance in your private life. Accomplish this by spending your time away from work with positive-thinking friends and family.

Are there positive-thinking people you'd like to have as friends? Why haven't you sought them out as friends? Don't let them get away, because their positiveness can't help but rub off on you. There's one serious warning though. If you have positive friends that bolster your self-esteem and help you out in difficulties - watch that this isn't a one-way street. Positive thinkers also need positive thinkers around them. If you're constantly draining them of their energy, you'll lose them as friends. Whining and complaining, then not doing anything about your complaints will cause them to back off from your company.

They too have difficult days. Don't dump your problems on their lap when this happens. Catch yourself when you feel the urge to state, *'You think you've had a bad day - wait till I tell you about mine!'* Your positive-thinking friends will run in the other direction.

One participant of my seminars wrote me to explain something that changed her workmates [including herself] from negative to positive thinkers. After attending my seminar, she asked her workmates to help her become a more positive-thinking person. She asked them to catch her whenever she was using negative thinking. This worked wonders for the whole group. They **all** began catching each other when they were using negative thinking. This change in behaviour soon became obvious to others. About a month later, their manager called them together and said, *'I don't know what you're doing differently, but please keep it up!'*

You can help workmates, friends and family by using this technique. Or ask them if they would like you to help them be more positive about life.

Unemployed people often find negative thinking cropping up, even if they're normally positive-thinking people. I've advised people who attend my 'Get That Job!' seminar that their attitude [positive or negative] would have a direct bearing on whether employers hire them or not.

In my role as Human Resources Manager, it was my responsibility to hire employees. I had two applicants applying for a position with my company. One stated she would do anything I needed and would take any job I offered her, because she really needed the job.

The other person gave me considerable information about her transferrable skills. These included - her ability to get along with others, her managerial skills and her attention to detail. After describing what she had to offer my company, she asked, *'Is there a position in your company that could make use of my skills and abilities?'*

Which of these two applicants would *you* hire? Would it be the one who was asking what *we* could do for *her* or the one who was asking what *she* could do for *us*? Of course, the more desirable candidate was the latter one and she's the one I hired.

Keep this in mind if you are unemployed and looking for work. Who would want a staff member who's constantly whining or complaining about their lot in life? Employers are looking for winners, not losers. They can afford to look around. If given the chance - wouldn't you give preference to the positive thinker?

Becoming a Positive Thinker

The most important assertive quality you can have is that of being a positive thinker.

> *'Positive thinkers believe they will succeed because ...*
>
> *Negative thinkers believe they will fail because ...'*

If your self-image is drooping, attend an assertiveness training class. Ask around, check course outlines and attend one that you think will meet your particular needs. If you're prone to negative thinking, you can help yourself to become a more positive thinker by doing the following:

1. Write down a list of people you associate with on a regular basis. Make three headings:
   a) Mainly positive thinkers
   b) Mainly negative thinkers
   c) Those who are right in the middle. [Don't have too many 'c' people - analyse them carefully to make them 'a's or 'b's if possible.]
2. Determine the percentage of time you spend with each person. (i.e.: If you spend seven hours a day with four work-mates, you'll probably spend about 20% each week with each of them. [You'll

have a total well over 100%, but don't worry about that.] For example, a partial list might show:

Positive: Mary: Percentage spent with her: 20%
Positive: Bob: Percentage spent with him: 10%
Negative: Sam: Percentage spent with him: 20%
Negative: Sue: Percentage spent with her: 15%
½ and ½: Barry: Percentage spent with him: 12%
½ and ½: Bill: Percentage spent with him: 20%

3. Determine whether you're spending more time with positive- or negative-thinking people.

Positive thinkers have the knowledge that:

'If you expect to fail - you will fail.

If you expect to win - you'll usually win.'

Positive thinking requires three prerequisites:

- Imagination,
- The ability to visualise, and
- The belief that you can do it!

Imagination

Imagination can be grouped into four sections:

1. Creative - generates ideas,
2. Anticipative - the ability to look ahead,
3. Visual - mind pictures - puts ideas together from descriptions,
4. Understanding - empathy for others.

Early conditioning often puts up barricades to stop us from using our imagination. Some may have been given the impression that to make a mistake was a 'sin.' Unfortunately, this has developed people who have tunnel-vision. These people refuse to take risks in case they make a mistake. They haven't learned that a mistake is just that - a mistake - nothing more. They should stop feeling guilty about making mistakes. Instead, they should vow that they won't make that particular mistake again.

The Ability to Visualise

Many a person's downfall comes when they try to change a bad habit by focusing on the undesirable behaviour. Instead, they should concentrate on the new behaviour that will take its place. We need expectations first, then need to visualise the fulfilment of our expectations. Most people miss the second one - they fail to visualise achieving their goal.

We use visualisation every day. When we want to wear a certain outfit, we visualise it while we search in the closet. If we're looking for a paring knife in the kitchen drawer, we picture how that paring knife looks. Learn to visualise the changes you wish to make, then do the hard work necessary to make your visualisations come true.

Most positive-thinking people use visualisation to help them achieve the goals they set in life. Many athletes use visualisation to see themselves win or do better than they have in the past.

Unfortunately, many women have been programmed to react as others expect them to. This is why many women have a difficult time in management positions. Other managers and executives of the company don't expect them to do well, so react accordingly. The very fact that the woman feels that management isn't behind her, makes her feel she can't succeed either. It takes strong will-power and the ability to visualise success for her to overcome this overt-conditioning that assumes she will fail.

Some believe that visualisation is a form of fantasising - living in a fantasy world. This isn't true. The person who uses visualisation correctly goes beyond dreaming or fantasising about something. The difference between visualisation and fantasy is as follows:

People who use visualisation see the final result. So do they who fantasise. The difference is that visualisers are more realistic, can see barricades in their way that will make reaching their goal a problem. After identifying the barricades, they will determine ways that will allow them to go over, under, around or through the barricade. Then they progress further in visualisation, possibly see another barricade and eliminate that one as well. Only if the barricades appear too big for the reward at the end, do they decide not to aim for the goal. In the process, they've saved valuable energy and time by taking a mental walk-through first.

Those who fantasise, just see the final results. Some, have unrealistic expectations and when they run into barricades say, *'Well, I guess I just wasn't meant to succeed at this,'* and quit. Others will keep plugging away, running into problem after problem and never stopping to determine if the result is worth the problems they must overcome.

Two Magic Questions

I used visualisation before I opened a branch office of my company in Maui, Hawaii. I was on a vacation from Canada, lying on the beach in Waikiki and kept having the thought, *'Would this ever be a wonderful place to work!'* I visualised working in Hawaii and took steps to see how I would go about doing so. My main barricade would be getting a work permit to work in the United States. As a Canadian citizen, this could be difficult, but not overwhelming.

Then I asked myself the two magic questions that I use to put everything into perspective. Ask yourself these two questions when you're trying to decide whether you should attempt something new:

> *'What have I got to gain by trying?*
>
> *What have I got to lose by trying?'*

If you have nothing to lose and a lot to gain - what's keeping you from trying it? What did I have to gain? I could work in paradise! What did I have to lose? Nothing. I decided to go for it. So, I got up from the beach and returned to my hotel room. Then [still in my bathing suit] I began phoning all the universities and colleges on the island of Oahu. Very soon I spoke with a representative of the University of Hawaii. He set up an appointment for me to see him the next day. At the interview, he offered me a contract to do a seminar for them the next spring on the island of Maui and they would look after the work permit! Shortly after, I opened my first branch office of my company in Maui.

How to be a positive thinker

Did you identify yourself as a negative thinker? There is hope - lots of it if you're willing to take the time and effort it requires to change bad habits into good ones. Remember that it will likely take three months of concentrated effort to stop yourself from slipping back into negative thinking. Are you willing to do that? If so, here are additional tips on how you can help yourself make the transition:

1. Get into the habit of writing down your bad thoughts about situations.

2. Identify when you're slipping into the *'I should have....'* or *'If only....'* rut. Analyse what negative feeling you're really having at the time. Is it depression, anger, frustration, jealousy, inferiority or any other negative feeling? Then determine the specific incident that made you have those feelings.
3. Ask yourself if you're overreacting or assuming something you haven't checked out with facts. Investigate carefully.
4. If you find you're drifting back to the way you used to act, remind yourself that this is **now** and change to a more positive way of looking at situations. Bring yourself out of the past – that's over. You can't change the past, but you can change the here and now as well as the future.
5. Make a detailed list of goals [see chapters 2 and 3] and start making your future happen. Don't overdo it. At first, give yourself simple goals to reach and increase the scope as you gain confidence in your abilities. Once you start testing your abilities, your mental computer will have more and more data upon which to decide whether you're likely to succeed or not. In the meantime, be ready to take a few knocks along the way.
6. Think of alternative ways you can accomplish tasks. Try to have Plan B and even Plan C on the back burner ready to call in, should Plan A not work out to your satisfaction. By no means - quit trying and give up in despair.

CHAPTER SEVEN

DEALING WITH MANIPULATION

Manipulating Others

You've made all your plans. You've set your goals and are slowly, but surely getting where you want to go. Then you run into 'manipulators' who get in your way at every turn. You feel frustrated and think about forgetting your goal. Then your defence mechanism kicks in, and you decide to fight back. But how do you fight a manipulator?

Positive Manipulation

There are two kinds of manipulation. Positive manipulation helps other people improve their lot in life. Most people use rational tactics including logic and bargaining to show they're willing to comply or compromise to find the best solution to differences, rather than use manipulation. They'll give up a little, if the other person will do the same.

Negative Manipulation

Negative manipulation is destructive, underhanded and sneaky. Manipulators use underhanded methods to get others to do what they want them to. They use power and control, giving the person the impression that they must, *'Do it their way or else ...'* Or they go out of their way to humble themselves, flattering the person, *'You're such a smart person, but couldn't we do it this way, just this once ...?'* Others may use ridicule, anger or shouting to meet their demands or through 'soft soaping' the other person.

Game Playing

People come in all shapes and sizes, and they also display many kinds of behaviour. The six major kinds of behaviour are:

- ❖ Passive
- ❖ Passive-resistant
- ❖ Assertive
- ❖ Indirect aggressive
- ❖ Aggressive

❖ Passive-aggressive

When people 'game-play' in their interaction with others, they use mainly passive resistance or indirect aggression. These games are manipulative and dishonest. They use indirect and unclear communication. Often the people playing the games aren't even aware that they're doing so. See if you can pick out any 'games' you play with others to get your way. If you do find any, please think of other more direct ways you could be communicating with others. I'll be using 'she' in my examples:

Passive Resistance

1. The sufferer - or *'After all I've done for you.'*

The sufferer gets what she wants by sending indirect messages. She may play the martyr, acts overworked, persecuted or totally dependent. She sighs a lot and utters indirect complaints. She's trying to say, *'If you appreciated me or even noticed everything I do for you - you'd want to do more for me.'*

If you must deal with this person, describe what you see her doing and ask that she be more direct when she communicates with you.

2. The uninvolved - or *'It doesn't matter to me, whatever you want.'*

Here's a sample conversation of a person who uses this game [Alice]:

John: *'Are you busy tonight? How about going to a movie?'*

Alice: [hesitating] *'Well ... I guess that's okay.'* [Her plans were to shop after work, eat her dinner and wash her hair.] *'Yes, that would be fun, I suppose.'* [weakly.]

John: *'What would you like to see?'*

Alice: *'Oh, it doesn't make any difference to me.'*

John: *'We could see the new science fiction down town or go to the western movie at the Varsity ...'*

Alice: *'Whichever you prefer.'* [She hates westerns.]

John: *'I don't feel like driving all the way down town, so let's go to the western movie.'*

Alice: [Long pause, followed by a sigh] *'Well ... okay.'*

John: [Gets the message] *'Are you sure that's what you want to do?'*

Alice: *'It doesn't really matter much - whichever you like.'*

The deliberately uninvolved person, is never wrong, but is never right either. Don't make others try to read your mind about what you really want. If you're dealing with this kind of person, explain what happens to you when they act indecisively [using feedback].

If you're the manipulator, others will soon tire of this kind of manipulative behaviour.

However, don't let the above stop you from saying, *'I don't really care,'* [if you really don't.] If you do have an opinion, say so.

3. *'I won't fight, but I won't give in either!'*

Helen [the manipulator] lives in the household of her son Bob and daughter-in-law Emily. Emily wants to re-decorate their family room by purchasing woven basket chairs with big pillows. They could use the pillows for sitting on the floor in front of the fireplace. Helen, [the mother-in-law] prefers a comfortable couch. The following conversation takes place.

Emily: *'Some of those fabrics on the pillows I saw yesterday are beautiful.'*

Helen: *'Are they made of cotton?'*

Emily: *'Yes they are.'*

Helen: *'They'll soon show the dirt, and they'll probably shrink when you wash them.'*

Emily: *'Well, maybe we could look for other kinds of fabric and cover them ourselves?'*

Helen: *'You should have that done professionally. Besides, anything that sits around on the floor will start looking terrible soon.* [Wearily] *But, if that's what you want, get them.'*

Emily: *'Well, I like big pillows. Is there anything you particularly want?'* [Leaving the door open for Helen to say what she really wants.]

Helen: *'Not exactly. Furniture should be sensible and made to last. But it's your house, do what you like, I can always sit in the living room.'* [Poor me!]

Later Helen reported to a friend that she was not the kind of mother-in-law who bothered her children with her opinions. Yet, Helen didn't support anyone else's ideas, unless they happened to be the same as hers.

Deal with this type of person by identifying that she is trying to manipulate you. For instance, Emily needs to talk to Helen about her manipulation and encourage her to be more direct when she's asked if she wants something done a particular way. When Helen tried to throw the guilt-trip on her, *'It's your house. Do what you like; I can always sit in the living room.'* Emily should have replied with, *'You're trying to make me feel responsible for how you feel. Why do you feel you would want to sit in the living room?'*

4. Saboteur - or *'I'll go through the motions - but fight you every step of the way.'*

Jane hates making coffee at the office, but rather than admit this to anyone, she makes lousy coffee. One time she uses half a package of coffee, then one and a half packages, hoping that someone else will do the job.

This is the kind of behaviour some children use when they're responsible for taking the garbage out. Parents may have to follow a trail of garbage down the sidewalk to the outside garbage can. The child thinks that if she does the job poorly enough, her parents will give the task to somebody else. If adults use this type of behaviour, it just makes them look very childish and inept at their work.

Deal with these people by making them repeat the task until they complete it satisfactorily.

5. Unwarranted fears

The fear victim is so ruled by anxiety and the fear that it arouses, that she avoids the situation and thus avoids facing the issue. She believes that dangerous or fearsome situations are cause for great concern, so she must continually think about them. This is irrational because worry or anxiety:

a. prevents an objective evaluation of the chance of a dangerous event,
b. will often keep the person from dealing with it effectively if it did occur,
c. may contribute to making it happen,
d. cannot possibly prevent inevitable events and,
e. makes many dreaded events appear worse than they are.

Potential dangers are not as catastrophic as they appear. Anxiety does not prevent them but may increase them. Worrying may be more harmful itself than the feared events. A university study showed that, of the events people fear;

- 40 per cent never happen.
- 30 per cent happened in the past.
- 22 per cent are needless, petty or small.
- 8 per cent are real, but divided into:
  - those the person could solve.
  - those the person can't solve.

Some people suffer from such problems as claustrophobia, agoraphobia, fear of heights, snakes, spiders, bees, the dark, being alone and of the unknown. If these unwarranted fears keep her from doing the activities she wishes to do or become overwhelming, it's time for her to seek professional help.

6. Sham or phoney assertive person

She pretends to be assertive, may even act open, warm and extroverted, but this is a cover-up for her lack of honesty. She's the person who would state, *'How wonderful to hear from you. I was just thinking about you.'* [Completely untrue - you know she detests you.] Behind your back, she takes pot shots at you. She has problems in any but the most superficial relationships. Others soon see through her untrue veneer and stay away from her.

If you're the recipient of her manipulation, confront her and state, *'If I've done something to offend you, please tell me. I don't like to hear second-hand that I've done something that has offended you.'* This teaches the person to deal directly with you, instead of talking about matters behind your back.

7. Everyone must love me!

Her goal is to have everyone - spouse, lover, children, boss, friends, shopkeepers and even the person who comes to the door selling magazines - to think she's the greatest. She hasn't learned that she can't please all the people, all the time. She feels fully responsible and guilty if a person doesn't like her. This is irrational, because it's an unattainable goal.

When dealing with this type of person, explain how impossible it is for her to please everyone. Help her understand that she shouldn't let others give her a good or a bad day. She can control how she responds instead of allowing herself to absorb the negative feelings.

8. Split Assertive Person

Most people use different behaviour styles that change with the situation. But this person may be a tiger on the job and a mouse in an intimate relationship or vice versa. She 'practices' assertiveness.

Suggest that she take an assertiveness training course, so she can identify which parts of her life are giving problems and change accordingly.

9. Dependent

She believes that she should be dependent on others and must have someone stronger on whom to rely. While we all depend on others somewhat, there's no reason to encourage dependency, for it leads to loss of independence, individualism and self-expression.

She's at the mercy of those who protect her. Dependency causes greater dependency. She fails to do things for herself or learn new skills and suffers from insecurity when her defenders are not available. She should strive for independence and responsibility and learn to refuse to accept help just because others offer it. Taking risks - that could possibly result in failure - are worth trying. Failing is not a catastrophe.

When an over-dependent person comes to you for help in making a decision - stop yourself from automatically stepping in to help. Instead ask her, *'What do you think you should do?'* Nine times out of ten, she'll know what she should do. She just wants confirmation. When she realises that she knew what to do all along, she'll see that she can make more decisions by herself.

10. Procrastinator

There are two approaches to tackling distasteful tasks. For example: Two employees have the same duties. Employee #1 gets all the unpleasant tasks out of the way at the beginning of the day and feels good at the end of her day. Employee #2 puts these tasks off as long as possible, getting testier as the day goes on, because she still has to complete the disagreeable tasks.

Another type of procrastinator says, *'I'll do it tomorrow.'* This is often the answer she gives when she's snowed under with work. She may not have time to complete the task, but grudgingly accepts it anyway. She needs to stand up for herself if she finds herself with too many tasks to complete and how to say *'No'* when necessary.

Occasionally, the procrastinator is a perfectionist who believes she must be competent at everything she tries. If she isn't, she doesn't consider herself a worthwhile person. This is impossible to accomplish because of a constant fear of failure. This results in feelings of inferiority and the inability to live her own life. She needs to learn how to enjoy the activity, rather than engaging in it solely for the results.

If someone asks you to do something you don't want to do, are you tempted to put the task off until you're ready to do it? Does this give you a sense of power over the situation? This is what most people do, and it can cause serious difficulty for them and others. Employees who consistently procrastinate when completing tasks, are often the ones who are the first ones fired. Companies can't afford to keep them on board. These employees look unprofessional, often become bottlenecks to others who are trying to get their work done and are a 'pain in the neck' to the more conscientious employees. Friends, family members and workmates normally don't tolerate her excessive procrastination either.

How can you tell when procrastination is becoming a problem? When you have something important to do, not much time to do it in, but find yourself looking for other activities to do instead. Or when you set deadlines and don't meet them! Procrastinators constantly delay making important decisions or work furiously at the last minute to complete crucial assignments.

There are five basic kinds of people who procrastinate more than average:

The Hurry-up Type: She waits until the last minute and then works around the clock to meet deadlines. She needs to set concrete deadlines of when she must have tasks completed, giving a little leeway in case she runs into problems.

I'll Decide Tomorrow: She postpones decisions until events resolve the situation or others force a decision upon her. She is normally a passive person who is a 'fence-sitter.'

Perfectionists: All tasks, no matter how small or insignificant she must complete faultlessly. She needs to select the tasks that are important and work hard at them. For the other assignments, she needs to know that it's okay *not* to do her best.

When dealing with a perfectionist, identify for her when she can complete something in draft form. Let her know that you're not expecting perfection from her.

I'll Show Them! She delays tasks others give to her, as a way of retaining a sense of personal power and control. An employee does this when a supervisor delegates a task she doesn't think she should be doing.

Muddler: She puts off work because of bad habits, poor organisation or lack of direction. She goes around in ever widening circles, accomplishing little and always has an excuse about why she hasn't completed a task.

11. Lateness

She is late for events she doesn't want to attend or is easily distracted and loses track of time. She often disrupts meetings, social events, concerts and lacks consideration for other people's valuable time.

There are three basic kinds of time users. For instance, if there was a 2 o'clock appointment:

- The (a) Person - She arrives at exactly 2:00 pm.

- The (b) Person - She arrives at 1:45 pm [and gives the impression that she just made it!]
- The (c) Person - She arrives at 2:15 pm [and act as if she's on time - gives no explanation for her lateness.]

The type (a) person often cuts a fine line between being on time and being late. Occasionally, she slips into the (c) group. The (b) person is on time, but may arrive too early, so wastes valuable time while she waits. If she feels the need to be at least fifteen minutes early for an appointment, she should bring work with her to do while she's waiting.

The (c) person doesn't comprehend why others are hostile towards her and doesn't understand why those who're waiting are upset. By her actions [coming in late] she's telling those who are waiting, that their time isn't important. She gives the impression that her time is more important; therefore, it's all right for others to wait for her.

If this type of person bothers you, confront her and tell her how you feel when she's late [use feedback.]

12. Always Slow

Sure, her report is ready, but it took her so long to prepare it, you felt like taking over for her. This type of person has low energy and often looks as if she's 'putting in time.' She exists rather than lives and is usually in a job she doesn't like. She can drive other more organised people to distraction.

If her actions affect you, identify what she's doing, give her deadlines and make her realise that you're counting on her to follow-through with the task. Explain the consequences she will face, if she does not do what you expected her to do [loss of your friendship - your co-operation in the future, etc.]

13. Avoidance

She believes it's easier to avoid certain difficulties and tasks than to face them. In truth, avoiding a task is often harder and more painful for her, than performing it. This can lead to later problems and dissatisfaction, including a loss of self-confidence. When she finds herself avoiding necessary responsibilities, she should analyse the reasons and find incentives to help her complete the tasks.

Treat this problem the same was as #12.

14. Sloppy or Careless

She completes the work so poorly, that someone else has to re-do her effort. This often takes more time than the original task. She has usually been in a 'rut' for so long that it will take considerable effort for her to 'dig herself out.'

Unfortunately, she doesn't perceive that she's in a rut in the first place. She plods along, day after day, year after year, often performing tasks she can barely tolerate. Her life is routine and mundane. She may not have considered there are other options open to her. This can happen generation after generation, because she hasn't had any other kind of role model.

Short of putting a bomb under her, there's not much you can do to get her motivated. Motivation has to come from within herself. Try solution in #12.

15. Live in the Past

She believes that her experiences must influence her present behaviour and that she can't make her future any different from her past. She may use this as an excuse to avoid changing her behaviour *'This is the way I am.'*

While it may be difficult to overcome past learning, it's not impossible. She needs to realise that the past is important but doesn't have to affect her future.

If life doesn't come up to her expectations [because of lack of insight on her part] console her with the idea that it's never too late for conditions to change. Although some opportunities of youth may have passed, each phase of life brings its own compensations for those who seek them. Instead of dwelling in the past, she needs to concentrate her energy on building a better, happier life and make the most of the present moment.

She may state, *'I'm too old ... I'm not smart enough ... I'm not good at that.'*

What she's stating is, *'I'm a finished product in this area and I'm never going to be different.'*

Deal with her by having a heart-to-heart talk with her where you identify her negative behaviour. Ask her permission to bring this behaviour to her attention if you hear her running herself down or reliving her past.

If it's you that's suffering from this problem, put a loose elastic band around your wrist and snap it [ouch] every time you catch yourself using this type of destructive behaviour.

16. Forgetfulness or neglect

Her usual comments are, *'Oh, I forgot.'* She expects others to remind her of tasks she should do, deadlines she must meet, who is responsible for what part of projects, etc. Other comments can be, *'Oh, I thought you were looking after that?'* Or *'I didn't know you wanted it for this Thursday.'*

Deal with this by asking for verbal and even written commitments from her.

Indirect Aggression

Those who play indirect aggression games use:

1. Sarcasm

Some sarcasm is nothing more than harmless kidding. It's non-threatening and can be a lot of fun. However, sarcasm can also be hurtful, designed to make others feel small.

The person using it feels a sense of power by watching other people squirm. Because it's no longer acceptable to hit a person with a fist, she hurls hurting comments instead.

She resorts to hurting sarcasm to express her negative emotions but is usually reluctant to identify the cause of her bad mood.

Hurtful sarcasm is one of the sneakiest, most manipulative and underhanded methods of getting one's way. The individual who uses hurtful sarcasm often doesn't feel very good about herself. This is why she tries to put others down to make herself feel more important. The sarcastic person wants others to get angry and defend themselves. The game continues when others respond defensively, or act hurt.

Examples of conversations using hurting sarcasm are:

'That outfit looks like it came off the ark.'

'You finally decided to honour us with your presence.'

'Ray did such a good job on his last project that the company demoted him.'

'If you're so smart, why aren't you my supervisor?'

'Can't you do anything right?'

'Oh sure, Mark's really smart ... he got 40 per cent on his last marketing exam.'

Who's in control of the situation when someone uses sarcasm? She is [the recipient of the sarcasm] until she replies. Should she respond to sarcasm with more sarcasm? No - because if she does, she'll just encourage more of the same. Instead, she should try to analyse why the person might feel the need to put her down. She should remind herself not to respond negatively to others' sarcastic remarks. Instead, she should try to get the person to stick to the facts. Once she has an idea of what really prompts the sarcasm, she can deal with the actual issue.

There's another tactic the victim could try. Rather than reacting to the person's sarcasm, she could turn it off by giving the person a blank look and continue doing what she was doing before the sarcastic remark. The giver of the sarcasm learns that the other person has not been tricked into defending herself. It's no longer fun to throw mean comments at her, so the sarcastic person will often look elsewhere for a new victim.

If the victim can't stay quiet [because she feels that the sarcasm warrants a response] she might say, *'Your last comment was very sarcastic and a put-down. Put-downs hurt. Can you explain why you said what you did?'*

Or *'Why did you feel you had to give me a put down like that?'*

O, *'That was a very sarcastic remark. What is it that you really want to say to me that you're covering up with sarcasm?'*

She needs to make the aggressive person account for her actions. Sometimes the sarcastic person isn't aware of how destructive her behaviour is to others.

The victim of the sarcasm must examine her actions too. Could she have done anything that triggered the person's sarcasm? Because sarcasm is often a defence mechanism, the giver of the sarcasm might have felt threatened. Could she have been careless, inattentive, late or unkind herself which made the person resort to sarcasm to get her point across?

If you're using sarcasm as a defence mechanism, ask yourself what is behind your sarcasm and deal with the issue with direct words - not sarcasm. Hopefully, you don't use manipulative sarcasm.

2. The Silent Treatment

Another form of indirect aggression is ignoring others, sulking, or giving them the silent treatment by refusing to discuss important issues with them. For example - Marie hadn't spoken to her workmate Betty for four days after an argument. They hadn't resolved the issue, although Betty had tried several times to get Marie to talk about the problem.

This is unfair and almost as destructive as vindictive sarcasm. This negative action is a no-win situation for both parties. Often the person giving the silent treatment wins the battle but prolongs the war. If she doesn't settle the issue by discussing it, it'll inevitably resurface later.

If you are the one faced with the silent treatment, make every effort to make the person understand that this is negative manipulation and 'dirty-pool.' It doesn't allow you to resolve the differences between the two of you and can escalate into a major blow-up. Say, *'I'm willing to listen to your side if you're willing to listen to mine.'* Then live up to your comment and really listen to the other person's side of the story.

3. Power Trips

'Power' is influence over other people or can just be not being dependent on others. The person who is overcome with her own power, stays pre-occupied with her own needs and is often oblivious to the wishes and desires of less powerful people.

She has trouble adjusting to how she should act when placed in a position of power. The employee who was formerly a worker and is now a supervisor or foreman may misunderstand her role. She may have seen other manipulative managers, who dominated and intimidated their staff. She hasn't identified that these managers usually feel inadequate themselves and cover up for this by displays of their strength and power.

When socialising, this kind of person is the one who treats service people like dirt. She does everything she can to make their jobs difficult yet complains if the person retaliates with less than his or her best service.

4. Gossip

Gossip is another form of indirect aggression and if vindictive enough can even be aggressive. When people pass on gossip from one person to another, it's inevitable that the meaning of the words changes somewhat from person to person. The person talking behind the back of other people doesn't allow them to defend themselves. For instance, a workmate states: *'Did you hear about Carmen's husband? The police picked him up for drunk driving last night.'*

How should she deal with the gossiper? She should either ignore the comments or suggest to the person that they both talk to Carmen about the information. To stop the gossip, she'd say to Carmen, *'I thought you should know there's a rumour going around that the police charged your husband with drunk driving last night. Were you aware of the rumour?'*

This lets Carmen know there *is* a rumour. She doesn't ask Carmen whether it's true - she just lets her know what's happening. The giver of the gossip soon learns that she won't get away with talking behind others' backs. It also stops gossipers from passing on unwanted gossip to this person.

5. Sticky-iffies

Sometimes individuals use sticky-iffies when giving compliments. This discounts her positive statement because she adds something negative to her comment as well. She may use disguised or obvious put-downs to hurt others. When dealing with her, use the following tactics:

1. After receiving the sticky-iffy or put-down, reflect your understanding of the situation. Say, *'You feel ... think ... believe ...'* which confirms that you heard what they said to you [a form of paraphrasing.]

2. Then state, *'I understand ... perceive ... appreciate ... empathise with ... realise ...'* then express their point of view as you perceive it.
3. State, *'I think ... feel ... believe ... have ...'* and state your beliefs about the topic. Don't start your statement with such words as but, however, although or nevertheless.
4. Ask an open question [one that can't be answered by a 'yes' or a 'no.']

For example, you would treat a discriminatory statement regarding age:

They say, *'You're pretty young to be a supervisor, aren't you?'*

You say, *'You feel that I'm too young to be a supervisor?'*

They say, *'Well you are young!'*

You say, *'I realise that I'm young. I have six years' experience in this department, have a B.A. degree and have completed all the supervisory training provided by my company. What other prerequisites do you feel I need to handle my position?'*

An example relating to racial slurs:

They say, *'Every time I take a taxi, it's always people from Asia who are driving. Can't you people find anything else to do, except drive a taxi?'*

You say, *'You feel that people from Asia should have jobs other than driving a taxi. I realise why you must believe that. Many people from my country must get extra education to work at their usual occupations, so become taxi drivers in the interim. I'm taking university courses and will soon be working in my normal type of occupation. What kind of special courses did you take to work in your occupation?'*

A gender-related example: They say, *'You're earning a good salary for a woman.'*

She says, *'You believe that women should earn less than men?'*

They say, *'Yes, I do.'*

You say, *'I appreciate what you're saying. I believe women deserve an equal chance to earn the same kind of salary as men. Women pay rent like men, pay the same for food as men and pay taxes like men. What are the reasons for your belief that women should earn less than men?'*

An example relating to a person's size:

They say, *'You're in pretty good shape for a man your size.'*

You say, *'You think that because I'm a smaller man, that I'm not strong?'*

They say, *'Well, you are small to be able to lift that big barbell.'*

You say, *'I can see how you could come up with that perception. I'm sixty years old now and have been lifting weights since I was fifteen. I've won several weight lifting contests and still work out every day. Can you see why I'm in good shape for a man my size?'*

Your tone of voice is very important in these exchanges. Your voice should not show defensiveness but should state facts. This starts a dialogue where you can discuss facts rather than emotions.

Use this technique for any sticky-iffy comments, disguised or obvious put-downs.

6. Tantrums

Adults who still resort to temper tantrums, haven't grown up. They use tantrums because they still get what they want if they yell and carry on. They love the control they have over others and enjoy watching everyone jump to do what they want.

If you must deal with a person who uses tantrums to get her way, try picturing her in an embarrassing situation. You could picture her as a squalling baby, wearing a clown outfit or naked if necessary. Humour can get you through many difficult situations. Somehow, when we're able to laugh about something, the tension lessens. Use funny mental pictures or even place a favourite cartoon near your desk to remind you to see the funny side of situations.

If she's resorting to tantrums, you should talk about her negative behaviour. State, *'That was a tantrum you just had. What were you hoping to accomplish by such childish behaviour?'* Refuse to give her special treatment to shut her up. If more people did this, she would stop her immature conduct. You may have to threaten to walk away from her if she acts in this childish way in the future.

If a friend, workmate, or family member has a tantrum:

a. Keep your cool and be firm. Make it clear to her that you intend to cool down the situation, before continuing your conversation.

b. Ask for facts about the problem.

c. Listen carefully and then do what you can to resolve the problem.

d. She may regret her outburst. Be ready to deal with her guilt feelings.

If you're the one resorting to this kind of self-serving behaviour, stop and analyse what others must think of your immature behaviour.

7. Lying

Some individuals that lie, can do so without batting an eye. These can be compulsive liars or 'con' artists who have told the same lies so often, that even they believe them. We can detect when others are lying by their non-verbal communication.

A person who's lying may hide her hands in her pockets or behind her back. Other signs are that she would:

- Avoid eye contact [usually look down.]
- Blink her eyes rapidly.
- Twitch and swallow repeatedly.
- Clear her throat and wet her lips.
- Shrug her shoulders.
- Rub her nose.
- Scratch her head while talking.
- Put a hand to the throat [more noticeable in women.]
- Rub the back of the neck [especially noticeable in men.]

If you see these signs, you have a good indication that she's lying. Most people who lie can't back up their lies with facts. So, when in doubt, ask her for facts.

8. Unwarranted guilt

Mary made a mistake and tried to forget about it, but others kept making comments that reminded her about it. She can't change the past despite how she feels about it! First, she needs to admit to herself and others that she did make a mistake. She shouldn't allow herself to become overwhelmed with guilt. Instead, she can learn from her experience. If an apology is necessary to remove the guilt - then she should apologise. Next, she should concentrate on tasks she did that she's proud of, instead of wallowing in guilt.

Sally's parents always expected her to become a teacher and made it clear that her choice to become an accountant was wrong. She needs to accept that she can choose to do or be something other than what others may expect or want her to be. It's nice to have others' approval, but not at the risk of her feelings of self-worth. She has the right to choose how she lives [providing she's not breaking the laws of the land.] However, she also must be ready to take the consequences of her behaviour and choices.

Some are bombarded by comments that are intended to make them feel guilty. For example:

'I work night and day to bring home my paycheque and you reward me by ...'

'I spent all day cooking this meal and it takes you fifteen minutes to eat it. The least you could do is help clean the table.'

'You never call me any more.'

'It's 3:00 am. How come you're so late? Are you trying to give me a heart attack?'

'If you loved me, you'd ...'

'What will the neighbours think?'

'You want Grandma and Grandpa to think you're bad mannered. Get busy and write those thank-you cards!'

'How can I believe you now when you lied to me last time you did this?'

'How can you just sit there watching your stupid football game when there's so much to do around here?'

'I stayed with your mother because of you kids.'

How can you handle people who're trying to make you feel guilty? First, you would identify which comments or statements were guilt laden. Then you'd respond by letting the manipulator know that you're aware of their manipulation. In the last instance:

'I stayed with your mother because of you kids,' you would reply, *'You've just tried to make me feel responsible for how you feel. Why do you feel that I was responsible for how you feel?'*

Stop Manipulation

When others try to shove you around emotionally, you should state how you feel. When others disapprove of what you do, it has nothing to do with what or who you are as a person.

Are you using positive or negative manipulation to get others to do things your way? Using positive manipulation to help someone become the best they can be is very acceptable, but negative manipulation, where you put your wishes first, is not.

You have no responsibility to make others happy - they make themselves happy. However, you should try to do anything you can, to help them along the way. Keep in mind that ultimately, you're responsible for your emotions - and they're responsible for theirs. You have the right to stand up for your rights and needs - just as they have the right to stand up for theirs. Your task is to find the middle ground between pleasing others and pleasing yourself.

Both positive and negative manipulation are effective methods to get others to do what you want, but negative manipulators often face retaliation from their victims. What tactics do you use when you're trying to persuade someone to do something? Do you try to manipulate others by using negative manipulation? Could others object to your manipulation?

If you see some of yourself here, work on being more direct in your communication with people.

'Don't count the days – make the days count!'

In his book ***'Games People Play,'*** Eric Berne describes some negative games people play to get their way. After reading his book, you'll likely pick out at least one game you play that's destructive to yourself and others. Those who manipulate others achieve a temporary sense of power over situations, but if others catch them playing games, they lose trust in them.

Or you might obtain a copy of my book ***Dealing with Difficult People.*** Chapter 2 is all about manipulation and identifies 115 ways people try to manipulate others and how to deal with those forms of manipulation.

CHAPTER EIGHT

OVERCOMING YOUR PAST

'Wherever you go, take your whole heart along.'

Dysfunctional homes

Men and women who've grown up in dysfunctional homes have tremendous barricades to overcome. These are families where we find child incest or where child and wife beating are the norm. As adults, these people don't really understand how 'normal,' families function. They have to guess and often revert to their memories of what to them was normal behaviour. Many people who have experienced family violence in their childhood accept violence as a method to resolve conflict. Therefore, family violence continues from generation to generation.

When children grow up seeing violence used to solve problems and manage stress, they learn that violence has a place in their families and believe that it's normal behaviour. If an assaulted mother remains in an abusive relationship and the father does not have to account for his violent behaviour, their children learn there are few consequences for violent behaviour.

Child Abuse

Cases where a stranger commits child rape or abuse, society deals with immediately and ruthlessly. But if a father, brother or mother commits the child rape or abuse, s/he rarely faces a jail term. If they receive a sentence, it's trivial when compared to stranger-child rape or abuse. This practice is criminal itself - the courts should consider child abuse to be child abuse no matter who assaults the child!

Physical and emotional child abuse is assault and assault is a crime. Assault is causing bodily harm to another person or threatening to harm a person. Although most people in society would agree with this, somehow it remains deaf and dumb when it's faced with cases of incest. The assault not only destroys a childhood and removes sexual innocence, but it sets the child up for a dysfunctional sexual future. These children have bruises on the inside and presently there are few laws in place to protect them.

Women who feel they must have a man at any price often stand by and allow their children to be abused with the excuses:

a) *'That's the way I was treated when I was a child.'* Many parents use this as their excuse to pass bad feelings on to their children. They believe their actions can't be wrong, so absolve themselves of the responsibility and consequences of their actions. They do not have to pass on their child abuse, but often if they don't receive professional help, that's exactly what happens.

b) *'He beats me too. I'm helpless.'* Adults make a choice to stay in an abusive relationship - children don't have this choice.

c) *'Where was I supposed to go - I have no money?'* Someone has to remove them, whether it's the other parent or society. That's what women's shelters are for.

d) *'My family turned their backs on me.'* Blaming your family is refusing to accept the responsibility that you're an adult now. It's very unlikely that your family will help you - if you too came from an abusive home.

One woman knew that her children's stepfather was sexually abusing them but chose to remain silent rather than face his wrath. She said, *'I was too embarrassed to say anything and let everyone know what was going on in our family.'* She allowed her 'embarrassment' of others finding out; overshadow her responsibility as a mother to do something about the situation. How could she be 'too embarrassed' to protect her children from her beast of a husband who was ruining their young lives?

Those who grow up in homes devoid of abuse, realise that this mother was as guilty as her husband, because she did nothing to end the abuse. In fact, her lack of positive action made it possible for that abuse to go on year after year.

Unfortunately, this mother had no inclination that hers was anything but a normal household. She was eleven the first time she'd been sexually abused. First it was her father, then later her brother who copied his father's unacceptable behaviour. This cycle goes on and on. If that family looked back two or three generations, they'd probably find that this was typical behaviour.

Not learned behaviour? Children learn violence from adults. Children learn to be victims from adults. Ask any shelter worker about three- and four-year-old boys who abuse their mothers, demanding juice, calling them 'Bitch,' and kicking them in the shins if they don't react immediately. Or they see tiny girls cringing when strangers speak to them. These children grow up to be abusers and victims and they repeat the cycle with their own children.

Child abuse can be one or all of the following: sexual abuse, incest, physical or emotional. The hidden child abuse is often verbal, rather than physical or related to a parent's unreasonable expectations of the child. Many parents unknowingly set their children up for failure by their verbal assaults on their children. They demonstrate this by undermining the self-esteem of the child through giving negative labels to them or unfairly comparing them to others. Those who were emotionally and verbally abused remember hearing such comments as, *'You're stupid, worthless and rotten.'*

Holly Love's story can be summed up in her poem entitled 'Love':

> *When I was three, I had a tom cat and his name was 'Sally.'*
> *He was a tough son of a gun and he taught me about love, softness and sensitivity.*
> *I didn't care that he was an old tom!*
> *When I was seven, I was a sweet little girl, and my Daddy called me 'Billy.'*
> *To gain his love, I was a tough little scrapper.*
> *He didn't know how to love a girl!*
> *I beat up the boys,*
> *I had mud ball fights and*
> *I chased away the love I sought.*
> *I learned to love like an innocent puppy,*
> *I ran for the ashtray, the slippers, the pipe,*
> *I lay down on the ground and I begged for love.*

Holly is the daughter of an alcoholic father. The poem came to her as she was participating in a course dealing with bottled-up emotions. She realised that her father had expected her to act like a puppy, demanding attention. Later, when she matured, she wanted to express her mature loving nature, she found it was difficult to alter her behaviour. She realised that her dad had only loved their dogs and she'd tried her damnedest to get his love and attention through playing by his rules of 'puppy love.'

Although she's now a successful businesswoman, the failure of two significant relationships made her realise that she needed some work in relating intimately with men. She began her healing journey in an Adult Children of Alcoholics group and moved on to the serious emotional job of changing her behaviour.

She hasn't established another serious relationship yet, but she sees daily progress when she relates with male friends. She knows it's only a matter of time until she's ready to become involved with a 'significant other.'

How to keep the cycle from repeating itself

We need a genuine and concerted effort by society, government, business, industry, education, medical and social agencies, individuals [you and me] to get at the root cause of violence and break the cycle.

It's often difficult for parents who were abused as children, to make the connection between their adult struggle with depression, substance abuse, low self-esteem, and their bad childhood relationships. Love and not being safe, seem to go together. If you don't have children but are a former child of abusive parents [verbal, physical, alcoholic and drug abuse] get professional help now. If you were an abused child and are now a parent:

a) Have the courage to acknowledge that you were abused.
b) Heal the damaged child inside yourself so you can become a well-balanced person and a good parent to your children.
c) Get professional help.

Healing is doing hard work on yourself to remove the pain and confusion. You must take responsibility for your own healing. Reclaim your personal dignity and when you do, your love and spontaneity will return, and your anger will dissipate. If you can heal those feelings in yourself first, you won't automatically pass bad feelings to your children when you're under stress.

If you're abusing your child now, get yourself to a facility that can help you control your impulse to abuse. Parents who abuse their children have made a choice **not** to heal and take care of themselves. Instead, they pass their legacy of pain and confusion from one generation to the next. They can break the cycle by healing themselves first.

Many parents wonder if they too may slip over the edge and become child abusers. These parents may have children who are truly difficult to handle. This child's negative behaviour includes aggressiveness, is whiny, picky, defiant, stubborn, loud, and disruptive in public. Some children are born that way and it's not their parent's fault. The child isn't working at being a difficult child. They're born with these traits that make them hard to raise. One or both parents were usually hard to raise themselves. Many of these children show the following characteristics. They:

- Are hyperactive, can't sit still for more than a few minutes at a time,
- Have short attention spans,
- Are easily distracted,
- Appear over-stimulated or oversensitive to their environment but are insensitive to the feelings of others,
- Withdraw from others,
- Are extremely moody,
- Seldom understand the consequences of their negative behaviour,
- Show stubbornness and persistence that things must go their own way,
- Cheat at games,
- Get into trouble at school and later with the law,
- Are perfectionists,
- Are easily frustrated,
- Show great disappointment even with small setbacks,
- Have problems adjusting to change of any kind.

These children can drive adults to distraction. To cope effectively, parents must first like their children. This differs from loving them. Liking their children, stems from acceptance of them as they are; with all their warts and behavioural patterns. This breeds patience, understanding and empathy in parents. Without this empathy the battle is likely to continue. Many parents admit they're on different wave lengths than that of their children. They don't understand why they do what they do and resort to control methods and punishment to get the errant child to behave. This seldom works and often triggers further negative behaviour from the child.

Some of these children are experts at pitting parents against each other. The parents' different disciplinary styles can in turn affect the child's sense of balance. Poor parental direction combined with the difficult behaviour leads to a vicious circle. Negative behaviour meets with negative reaction and the participants become locked into a consistent negative situation. Both parents and children feel as if they're victims. The tension the child initiates can cause the marriage to flounder.

How are parents to deal with this kind of situation?

Try to understand why your child acts the way s/he does. Communicate - have dialogue with your child. Don't make the interview an inquisition where you back them into a corner making them explain why they do what they do. Often the child doesn't know why either.

Set guidelines the child can meet. Discuss these guidelines with the child and get his or her input about where s/he would like some leeway. Read everything you can about manipulation and the games people play to get their way. Learn coping tactics to overcome negative reactions to game playing.

Try to remain objective. Deal with the child rationally, rather than emotionally. Walk away from the situation if necessary until you've calmed down. Putting the child in isolation in the meantime might be best for you both. Make sure the child understands that you aren't abandoning them but will discuss the problem later when you've both calmed down. In the meantime, write down what the child has done, how you felt about it and what you're willing to do about it. You'll have to determine the consequences of the child's actions and be ready to follow through.

For instance, if Johnnie hits his brother, tell him that he can't watch his favourite television program if he does it again in the future. Try to teach him how to deal with the situation that led up to his hitting his brother. Communicate, listen and be willing to hear his side of the situation.

If you find you can't change the negative behaviour, discuss the problem with a child psychologist or get family counselling so the whole family can deal with the child's difficult behaviour.

Wife Battering

Wife battering is also a crime. Every citizen has the right to freedom from assault or from fear of assault. Wife assault involves the husband intimidating his wife, either by threat or by actual use of physical violence. He may direct his violence at her person or her property. The purpose of the assault is to control her behaviour. Sometimes the fear of violence is enough to establish control. Underlying all abuse is a power imbalance between the victim and the offender.

Abuse can be in the form of physical, sexual, psychological, destruction of property or pets and financial dependency. The longer the violence continues, the greater the chance is that the victim will experience all five forms of abuse. Survivors of wife assault, state their financial dependence on their partners was one of the main reasons for staying in the abusive relationships. Almost half of all homicides are between spouses and most of the victims are women.

It's estimated that there are ten unreported cases for every call by a battered wife to the police. Wife beating crosses all income and geographical lines. It spans all ages, races, nationalities, and educational levels. It's seldom a one-time occurrence. Most battered women are beaten regularly, and beatings often increase in frequency and severity. Beating can lead to permanent physical and mental disability or death. It seldom gets better without treatment.

While alcohol and drug abuse are factors in about half the cases of beatings, many men are sober when they assault their wives. And not all drinking or alcoholic men batter their wives.

Most women are beaten for no reason - and often without warning. Stress, conflict, arguments, quarrels and differences are part of any relationship. Pregnancy - added family responsibility and employment problems are key stress factors. Anger and frustration may result, but violence is never an appropriate answer.

Battered wives stay in relationships for many reasons. Many hope to change a man they love. At other times, he may be genuinely penitent, loving and generous. Women may feel they're to blame and try to change. They don't want to admit the marriage is a failure. They feel unloyal, ashamed, isolated, or unique, but most of all, women stay because they have nowhere to go. They feel trapped.

Both men and women abuse their children and spouses, but studies show that many more men do so than women. Most men would argue that not all men are violent, and that society shouldn't judge all men because of the actions of the men who are. Unfortunately, many of the men who condemn violence, abuse their wives and children because they don't consider their actions as being violent.

The belief has been drummed into them, that men have the right to dominate women and thus if they wish, they can abuse them. Fathers tell their sons, *'You can't hit your sister - she's a girl.'* Millions of these small boys hear such comments from a father who then turns around and beats their mother, because supper is late.

Not too long ago, British Statutory law still allowed a man to beat his wife, provided he used a stick no thicker than his thumb - which is where the phrase 'rule of thumb' comes from. Battered wives don't stay in abusive situations because they like it, but because they've come to believe that:

- They could never get a job,
- That no other man would want them,
- They could never survive on their own,

[And the big one:]

- They deserve the abuse because they're so stupid and ugly.

Leonore Walker's book *'The Battered Woman'* shows three distinct phases in wife battering:

a) The Tension-Building Phase.
b) The Battering Phase.
c) Remorse and Contrite Phase [The Honeymoon Phase.]

Both partners require extensive counselling to make their marriage work. If they don't - the abusive man will seek another woman and continue the cycle. Often, the man believes that he has the 'right' to beat his wife because that's all he's learned from his father's behaviour.

Women's safety should not be a function of male dominance, but a woman's inherent right to safety. It's unfortunate that society's emphasis seems to be on protecting women, instead of on curing the men who abuse them.

For instance, when a man beats his wife, instead of society forcing him to vacate the home, his innocent wife and children must do so, often forcing them to live in crowded women's shelters.

How to stop wife battering and child abuse

How do people who've grown up in that type of environment deal with it? They must first want to stop what's happening. Then they'll:

- ✓ Remove themselves from the situation [being together is poison and they'll both return automatically to the way they behaved before]
- ✓ Move to a safe place where they can get self-help,
- ✓ Realise that the transition from being dependent or battered, to one of deciding for themselves will take time - it won't happen overnight.
- ✓ Get help for their children, who can't help but be affected,
- ✓ Surround themselves with a strong support network, and
- ✓ Take responsibility for themselves and their actions.

Action is the only way out of the situation. In addition:

1. They must get qualified medical help to learn how to deal with the horrific guilt feelings that cling to a person who has had to submit to such aberrant behaviour. They must believe that they were innocent victims of the abuse.
2. They must learn how normal families really function. They learn this by observing and talking with friends whose families display normal nurturing, loving behaviour. They would ask questions of close friends and seek their help in identifying any reactions to situations or behaviour they're portraying that appears different from how they perceive life.
3. Then they need to put their past behind them. What happened in the past - is in the past. They need to stop letting it influence everything they do and learn to stop themselves when they find themselves slipping into their former negative thinking.
4. They need to set specific realistic goals for themselves and keep telling themselves that they will succeed.
5. Write down and remember their successes. They would bring out their 'brag list' whenever they're having serious doubts about whether they can succeed or not.

Where can women go for emergency help? Women's shelters have sprung up all over the country. They:

a. provide a temporary shelter for women and children who are victims of emotional or physical domestic violence.
b. offer a secure and supportive atmosphere where a woman can decide for herself her family's future.
c. give information and referral to community agencies that help women make choices that are best for them.

How can friends help battered women and their children?

1. Listen to her - be supportive and understanding. Let her know she's not alone or to blame. Don't be judgmental.
2. Suggest she go to a doctor as soon as possible following a beating. She should tell the doctor the cause of her injuries because she may need medical evidence later. Coloured photographs of her injuries may be vital evidence in court. If you witnessed the battering or saw her directly afterward; be willing to act as a witness in court.
3. If she plans to leave home, remind her to take legal identification such as social insurance or security card, driver's license, credit cards, birth certificates [hers and her children's], marriage certificate and any medical documents required. She should also know her husband's social insurance number, tax file number and his driver's licence so she can trace him to get child support.
4. If she doesn't know what to do, refer her to a women's shelter. You can help her to start a new life by helping her find a job, housing and child care.

Remember, what she does is her decision. It's her life. Many women have been in this situation and have made new, violence-free lives for themselves. Regardless or her decision, remember she needs emotional support during this difficult period in her life.

Adult Rape Victims

Rape, whether it's of a male or a female is a terrifying act to the victim no matter at what age the outrage took place. Most suffer from post-traumatic stress disorder (PTSD) at least in the beginning. Almost 20 per cent of raped women never completely get rid of their PTSD symptoms.

Victims who felt they were in great physical danger during the rape were more likely to get severe PTSD than those who felt they were in less danger. If threatened with a weapon or raped by a stranger, they were more likely to get severe PTSD. Date rape often carries more physical violence for women. This is because the woman has a greater sense of security. After all, she knows the man and she's more likely to resist and fight back. The result can be a severe beating.

Others felt they had set themselves up for rape by 'doing something dumb' so suffered from feelings of guilt and shame. Those who were raped when they felt they had 'done everything right' suffered greater anxiety because they saw the world as an unsafe place.

Some victims don't tell anybody because they're afraid others will blame them for the rape. They have not compared their assault to other crimes. For instance, nobody would believe that they had 'asked for it,' if they were the victims of a robbery or if they were physically assaulted. Nobody wants to hear about a rape. The message seems to be, 'Don't talk about it.'

How victims can be assisted:

Experts in this area advise that helping the victim re-experience the rape by talking about it, imagining it, re-creating it in the mind, is the best treatment. Most reveal that they have recurring nightmares, flashbacks, and endless thoughts of how they could have handled the event better.

After a few weeks, most can resume near-normal lives. They're better prepared to deal with issues that were frightening to them, such as going to places that they perceive as threatening or sleeping alone in their homes.

After the initial period where they talk out their feelings and memories of the event, they can replace the negative thoughts with pleasant ones. The rubber band on the wrist is a helpful technique. When they find themselves dwelling on the event, they snap the band, which gives their sub-conscious mind a jolt to keep it from going back to the negative thoughts.

Getting instruction on how they can manage future anxiety. For example, they may have to deal with sudden anxiety, if they see someone who resembles the criminal who committed the crime.

Offering counselling to help the victim handle everyday events.

Battling Spouses

Everyone's human and most people 'fly off the handle' at one time or another with their spouses. A husband may wonder if he might batter his wife if he was mad enough. Because of their nearness to each other, couples may find that their disagreements turn out to be shouting matches where neither member seems to hear the other person's side of the dispute. This often results in louder and louder responses until one member storms off in a huff, while another may resort to pouting and withdrawal. This can result in a vicious circle of conflict.

It's unfortunate that couples wait until one or both are considering separation or divorce to get marriage counselling. When couples face the threat that the quality of their marriage is in jeopardy, they need help. If they'd been aware of a workable communication technique early in their marriage, the situation might not have reached the stage where their marriage was in trouble.

How to resolve battles between spouses

This communication technique involves trust and faith in each other. Use it when communicating with intimate friends and relatives. Participants abide by the 'rules' and see it through.

The ideal time to discuss this technique with your partner is when both are in a co-operative mood - before the conflict happens. It won't work if you're already steamed up. So discuss this technique before you have a blow-up.

Have a signal you can use, such as holding your hand up to signify that you want to use the technique. Both must abide by the rules for it to work. This is how the process works:

1. One person calls a meeting with the other and asks permission to express his or her negative feelings.
2. Only one person talks at a time - the other does nothing but listen and absorb the information until called upon to act.
3. Before the meeting, Person (a) tries to identify what negative childhood tape may be playing [if any] that made them feel badly about the other person's behaviour.
   [Note: Most negative reactions to behaviours of others are reactions from situations that have happened to them as children.]
   i. Person (a) will tell person (b) how s/he feels about issues or something the other's doing that's causing him/her negative feelings.
   ii. Person (b) will nod to show they understand but not argue or say anything.
4. Person (a) makes such statements as, '*I feel ... when you do ...*' then explains what s/he wants from the other, '*I need you to ...*'

5. Person (b) then paraphrases as closely as possible, what s/he heard the partner explain about the situation, his/her feelings and what s/he wants from him or her.
6. Person (a) confirms or corrects the information.
7. Person (b) tells Person (a) how s/he feels about what's been said and how s/he intends to deal with it.
8. After Person (a) feels comfortable that s/he's settled the issue, Person (b) may identify one of their relationship problems. The process continues until they resolve all outstanding problems.

There's another way to use this process. One partner would still give the signal [raised hand?] then:

1) Write down their side of the story.
2) Toss a coin to see who talks first. The person winning the coin toss speaks first.
3) The former listener now becomes the speaker, and the new listener follows the same instructions.

The couple needs to make a commitment that they will concentrate carefully on what the other person is saying, otherwise the process won't work. They should refrain from formulating any answer to the conflict until it's their turn to speak.

Couples who have used the above procedure find that they truly hear what the other person is saying, [sometimes for the first time.] This occurs because they aren't concentrating on formulating their answer. Instead, they concentrate on the other person's side of the story, using empathy to try to understand how the other person really feels about the dispute. The result is open, honest communication between the couple, which settles most conflicts.

It's possible the one or the other person is so worked up that they can't discuss the problem right away. They would ask for time to calm down before discussing the problem. But they should discuss the problem at the first opportunity - they mustn't procrastinate!

There may be other times in conversations where both partners are in strong disagreement about something such as: abortion, capital punishment, religion, politics, etc.

Let's say the couple have discussed their opposing views and try valiantly to sway the other person to their point of view. As the debate continues, it's obvious that neither is going to budge from their views. Only in issues of this magnitude, should one of them state, *'You're entitled to your opinion and so am I. It looks as if neither of us is going to change our opinion, so I suggest we drop this topic and not discuss it any more.'*

Dealing with Divorce

When spousal conflicts escalate, they often lead to separation and divorce. How do the partners fare after divorce? It often depends on who left whom as to who keeps their self-esteem intact. Many give their divorce as a reason for their low self-esteem level, because they feel they're failures.

How do most men cope with divorce? More men than women have problems dealing with divorce. They're more likely to focus more on the existing task, than deal with the emotions that go with it. Men struggle with divorce because they're not sure why it happened. Many feel lost and adrift, because everything in their personal lives changes. No longer do they have someone to look after their everyday needs.

If they don't have custody of their children, they suffer emotional stress because they see their children less frequently. Many go home to a new environment - alone. The silence is deafening, one man explained. Men seldom read such articles as *'How to make your marriage work'* unless they face severe marital difficulties and by that time - it's usually too late.

Men are less willing to accept help from professionals with their problems. They won't or can't admit they need help and some don't have the support network needed in crisis situations such as this. To cope, many men revert to alcohol or become workaholics. This does little to overcome their depression and confusion. They have a higher rate of admission to psychiatric hospitals and are more successful at suicide.

Men move into new relationships before they finish the old one, which brings new problems. Once married, men are more dependent upon staying married than women. Strong feelings of attachment last long after separation and divorce. They go through the same stages as grieving - denial, mourning, anger and finally acceptance.

The visiting father may face confusing messages from his children who are going through their own kind of grief. They may withdraw from him, sulk, be angry or show defiance. Some feel abandoned and may refuse to see him. The more involved a father remains with his children after divorce, the healthier he'll be emotionally and the stronger the bond will remain with his children.

How do women deal with divorce? Women are more willing to accept professional help with problems during a family break-up. They're more likely to seek help because they're often more people-oriented than men. For many women the biggest adjustment is financial. Those who have stayed at home with their children may face the sudden [and often unexpected] reality that they must go out and work. This can be devastating to some who're still struggling with the adjustment of divorce. Many become overwhelmed with the sheer size of their responsibilities. Some have never balanced a chequebook; know how to do preventive maintenance on their car, appliances and household repairs. They deal with children who are themselves inundated with the changes that often results in serious behaviour problems.

On the brighter side, because women more often initiate separations and divorce, they find that they recuperate sooner. Most have a stronger social network of family and friends for support. Many women find the quality of their life improves. They take longer to re-establish relationships with men. They're more cautious, because of the risks in dating and the chance of rape.

Women read more about how to keep their relationship healthy and see the signs of deterioration of the marriage long before the husband usually does.

A man for every woman - a woman for every man

Many people feel lonely and alone. This affects their entire life and future happiness. Many give up hoping that they might find the 'ideal' mate. The following dispels that myth:

- ✓ *'For every woman who's tired of acting weak when she knows she is strong, there's a man who's tired of appearing strong when he feels vulnerable.*
- ✓ *For every man who's burdened with the constant expectation of 'knowing everything, there's a woman who's tired of acting dumb.*

- *For every woman who's tired of being called an 'emotional female,' there's a man who is denied the right to weep and be gentle.*
- *For every man who finds competition the only way to prove his masculinity, is a woman who's called unfeminine when she competes.*
- *For every woman who's tired of being a sex object, there's a man who must worry about his potency.*
- *For every man who's denied the full pleasure of shared parenthood, there's a woman who feels 'tied down' by her children.*
- *For every woman who's denied meaningful employment or equal pay, there's a man who must bear the full financial responsibility for another human being.*
- *For every man who has the satisfaction of cooking, there's a woman who understands the intricacies of an automobile.*
- *For every woman who takes a step toward her own liberation, there's a man who finds the way to freedom has been made a little easier.'*

(Adapted from a brief from the Centre for Woman and Religion, Berkeley, California.)

Are you still blaming others?

Are you using your past or blaming something or someone else for what's happening in your life right now? Are you blaming your childhood or an abusive relationship for how you behave now? If so - have a serious talk with yourself and stop doing it! Don't let others from your past influence how you spend your future - that belongs exclusively to you. Look after yourself and get professional help if you're having problems letting go. Don't make excuses - take command of your future - no one else can do it for you.

CHAPTER NINE

HOW TO DEAL WITH YOUR NEGATIVE EMOTIONS

*'The world is like a mirror. If you face it smiling,
it smiles right back!'*

Life for most of us goes on day after day, bringing with it its usual number of trials and tribulations. Sometimes these troubles pile up and we react physically, mentally or emotionally. It's important to identify when we're in trouble.

Early signs of emotional problems

[Used with permission of Canadian Mental Health Association]

Minor emotional upsets are as natural as the common cold or headache. And they can strike anyone. Now and again we all lose our cool, feel inferior and suffer from guilt. Learning to control our emotions is part of character development.

Many times, emotional and personality problems have little or no ill effect on a person's actions, thoughts and feelings. But, when problems and difficulties continue and the upset feelings keep coming back, self-esteem suffers.

When this happens it's helpful to recognise some signs that identify that more serious trouble may be ahead unless they do something to relieve the stressors.

Listed below are eleven recognisable signs, but it's important to make a sensible assessment. There's no need to rush off to a doctor at the first sign of a headache or vague feeling of being out of sorts with life.

1. Withdrawal. Signs are:
   - Being afraid to face the chance of failure and, as a result, escaping repeatedly to movies, watching television, drinking excessively,
   - Finding responsibilities of marriage, children or work too difficult to face.

2. Belligerence:
   - Being quarrelsome - continually or repeatedly for almost no reason at all.
3. Self-centredness:
   - Being unable to share material possessions, time, friendship or advice with others, - being selfish, putting yourself first in everything and believing the world revolves around you.
4. Suspicion and mistrust:
   - Believing that the world is full of dishonesty, disappointments, obstacles and frustrations and nothing else, trusting no one, Feeling that people are waiting for an opportunity to cause difficulty or are out to get you or 'take you for a ride.'
5. Insomnia:
   - Repeatedly not being able to sleep, - Permanently tired and slowed down,
   - Finding it hard to wake up in the morning even after a good sleep,
   - Refusing to get out of bed at the risk of losing employment and,
   - Neglecting family.
6. Anxiety:
   - Worrying excessively about everything,
   - Very apprehensive of the future,
   - Afraid of making decisions, large or small.
7. Day dreams and fantasy:
   - Spending too much time imagining how life could be, so that you forget the good part of life,
   - Locking out problems that come along, not seeing them,
   - Living in another world.
8. Hypochondria:
   - Worrying excessively about minor physical ailments,
   - Imagining sickness and ill health, being certain of suffering from some particular illness that is clearly non-existent.
9. Poor emotional control:
   - Indulging in frequent temper tantrums,
   - Becoming very excitable over matters of little importance, exaggerating angry outbursts beyond reason.
10. Excessive moodiness:
    - Feeling low and depressed nearly always,

- Feeling that nothing is worth doing,
- Have even considering taking your life.

11. Helplessness and dependency:
    - Letting others make decisions - even small ones,
    - Letting others do everything for you,
    - Unable to be alone,
    - Procrastinating excessively.

Sometimes related emotional disturbances cause physical symptoms and illnesses. These range from migraine headaches to obesity and diabetes.

Remember that just being aware of a sign or two does not always mean you're ill. Far from it, for many of the milder symptoms, it may be enough to find a sympathetic person to listen. This could be your doctor, a relative, friend or social worker. For more serious problems, contact the family doctor. S/he is in the best position to help and to make a referral to a specialist if required.

Getting over the 'Holiday Blues'

Feelings of being alone or abandoned at a time where there's been a loss of an important relationship can be magnified during holiday seasons. Try to build into the holiday the activities from your past that brought you pleasure. Know that the holiday is not going to be the same as it used to be. Construct a new ritual to replace your old one. Find new ways of celebrating it, something that's meaningful and worthwhile. For instance, invite others who're alone for the holidays to join you for a meal or for an evening together.

Another reason many people feel blue at holiday time, is because the hours of sunlight may be shorter. Spending more time in the sunlight can usually help. If this isn't available, read for a few hours each day in front of a special light. Its wavelength mimics natural sunlight to achieve the same effect as outdoors. [Please note that these are not sunlamps or tanning lamps.] Results are best if the light strikes the front of your forehead, and your eyes are open. Even sleeping under it for a couple of hours will help.

Tensions; how to live with them:

[Permission given by Canadian Mental Health Association]

Tension and anxiety are our normal reactions to defend against threats to our safety, well being and happiness. Accidents, violence, financial trouble, job problems, family relations often cause a normal increase in anxiety and tension.

Sometimes, however, we become overly tense and anxious when no real danger exists. We become frazzled and on edge - unable to reason things out or control our feelings. This is a time to be watchful.

Below are 11 steps you can take to deal more effectively with your tensions. You'll need persistence and determination, but the results will be worth it.

Remember that on matters of health, your physician is your best guide. Follow his or her instructions carefully.

1. Talk it out.

When something worries you, talk it out. Sit down with a level-headed person you trust: husband or wife, father or mother, good friend, clergyman, family doctor, teacher, school counsellor. Talking helps to relieve strain and enables you to see the problem more clearly.

2. Escape for a while.

Often it helps to escape from the problem for a short time: lose yourself in a movie or book, take a drive in the country. It's realistic to escape punishment long enough to recover breath and balance. But be prepared to come back and grapple with the problem when you're more composed.

3. Work off your anger.

While anger may give you a temporary sense of righteousness or even power, it will probably leave you feeling foolish. If you have the urge to lash out, wait until tomorrow. Do something constructive with that pent-up energy - spade the garden, clean out the garage, play a game of tennis and take a long walk. A day or two later you'll be better prepared to deal with the problem.

4. Give in occasionally.

If you find yourself getting into frequent quarrels and feeling defiant, remember that frustrated children behave the same way.

Stand your ground but do it calmly and remember that you could be wrong. Even if you're dead right, it's easier on your system to give in now and then. You'll relieve some tension and have a feeling of satisfaction.

5. Do something for others.

If you find that you're worrying about yourself all the time, try doing something for someone else. The steam will go out of your own worries and instead you'll have a good feeling.

6. Take one thing at a time.

For people under tension, an ordinary work-load may seem unbearable. The tasks loom so large that it becomes painful to tackle any part. To sort your way out of it, take a few of the most urgent tasks and pitch into them. Leave everything else aside. Once you've cleared a few away, the others won't seem such a 'horrible mess.' You'll be into the swing and the balance of the work will be easier.

7. Shun the 'superperson' role.

Some people expect too much of themselves; they strive for perfection in everything they do. The frustration of failure leaves them in a constant state of worry and anxiety. Decide what you do well and put your major effort in this direction. These are probably things you like to do, hence ones that give you the most satisfaction. Then, perhaps, tackle the ones you can't do so well. Give them your best, but don't berate yourself if you don't achieve the impossible.

8. Go easy with your criticism.

Expecting too much of others can lead to feelings of frustration and disappointment. Each person has his or her own virtues, shortcomings, values - his or her own right to develop as an individual. Instead of being critical, search out the other's good points and help him or her to develop them. This will give both of you satisfaction and help you gain a better perspective of yourself.

9. Give the other person a break.

People under emotional tension often feel they have to 'get there first' – to edge out the other person. It can be something as common as highway driving. Competition is contagious, but so is co-operation. When you give the others a break, you often make things easier for yourself; if they no longer feel you are a threat to them, they stop being a threat to you.

10. Make yourself 'available.'

Many of us have the feeling that we're being left out, slighted, neglected and rejected. Often, we just imagine that other people feel this way about us. They may be waiting for us to make the first move. Instead of shrinking away and withdrawing, it's much healthier to continue to 'make yourself available.' Of course, the opposite - pushing yourself forward at every opportunity - is equally futile. This can be misinterpreted and lead to real rejection. There is a middle ground. Try it.

11. Schedule your recreation.

Some people drive themselves so hard that they allow themselves almost no time for recreation - an essential for good physical and mental health. Set aside definite hours for a hobby or sport that will absorb you completely. A time to forget about work and worries.

How to handle a panic attack

We've all suffered from sweaty palms and the pounding heart that anxiety initiates. This could be before a meeting with our supervisor, before a date with someone special or while waiting to see our doctor for results of medical tests. This is normal behaviour, which is part of our fight/flight response to tension.

Unfortunately, millions of others experience the more serious and often paralysing form of anxiety. Some people describe their fear that they may be losing their mind or dying. This is a panic attack that is much more severe than a simple anxiety attack. These attacks can be as short as a few minutes to several hours. They normally build to a peak then dissipate, leaving the person exhausted and shaken. The episode is even more frightening because it can come on for no apparent reason.

Panic attacks are often generic - others in the family also suffer the same fate. Negative childhood memories [especially those related to separation from a loved one] cause others. Some only have one attack; others are prone to repeated attacks. Twice as many women as men suffer from this disorder.

Many sufferers are perfectionists, eager to please others and get their sense of value from what they can do for others rather from their own sense of self-worth. Stressful events can trigger an attack. Something as simple as having too much caffeine in their diet can cause the blockage of receptors in the brain.

How can one cope with this type of attack?

a) Force yourself to breathe as normally as possible. Most victims appear to hold their breath as they would if they were startled or approached by a wild animal. This can cause a light-headed feeling and a feeling of powerlessness.

b) Do something that can jolt you out of your attack. Popular ways are to snap a rubber band on your wrist, list in your mind the number of relatives you have or count the number of heartbeats you can feel. Do anything that can focus on something other than your attack.

c) Tell someone you trust what's happening – don't feel you have to hide it. A loving touch from someone you care about can help you return to reality.

d) Try not to get away from the situation otherwise you will associate that place with negative thoughts. Stay till your attack is over, so you know you can return to normal in that setting. If you stay, the attack will pass and if you have another one, you'll remember that, as frightening as it was, that nothing drastic happened. Often the biggest problem for sufferers is not getting on a plane or doing their shopping, but the fear that they may have another panic attack.

When should you seek professional help? If you find you can't stop thinking about your attacks or you've had at least one attack a week for several weeks, you may be suffering from a panic disorder. A complete physical exam is first and then see a mental-health professional who's familiar with anxiety and phobia attacks who can get you back on track.

Anger

People have many ways of expressing anger. Many are destructive, not only to the angry person, but to those around them. I compare allowing your anger to let you lose control to being an emotional strip tease. You'd never take your clothes off in front of a stranger, then why would you let them see your inner feelings. Also, when a person is angry, they often behave irrationally. Anyone acting irrationally is temporarily insane. If you're dealing with an angry person and you respond with anger, all you have is two people having an insane conversation.

Anger is shown in many ways such as:

- Yelling at or blaming others,
- Verbal abuse - sarcasm or ridicule,
- Physical violence,
- Threats to others,
- Temper tantrums,
- Silent treatment or withdrawal,
- Denial,
- Vandalism,
- Drugs and alcohol.

Anger: the 'Mystery' Feeling

[Permission given by Canadian Mental Health Association]

What's all the mystery about? The mystery is not anger, the feeling itself, but the many ways in which people let it out or hold it in or twist it until it becomes something else. And part of the mystery is how far we go to convince ourselves and others that anger does not exist.

'Sometimes things and people can really get me fried.'

We get angry when we're disappointed about something. Anger happens in us when we notice a gap between what we want or need from the world or someone we care about and what we're getting. It can also result from a sense of loss, such as a loss of someone through death or divorce or the loss of health, a job or a cherished possession. Anger is a signal that we are facing a frustrating or stressful situation. Like traffic signals or road signs, anger and other feelings are there to help us get over the humps and around the roadblocks that are a part of everyday living.

Anger and love for example, may not seem to have much in common on the surface. But both are very powerful and most satisfying when they can be felt and expressed in similar ways - openly and honestly. Far too often, anger is not expressed openly and that's where the problem begins.

'Anger has a way of sneaking out as something else.'

For instance: You say you're bored? Maybe what you really are is angry because you seem to be missing out on something.

You say your sex life is not what you would like it to be? Consider how difficult it is to make love to someone you're angry with - or someone who's angry with you.

You can put anger off, hoping it will go away. You can turn it into something else, like over-eating, over-drinking or over-working. You can become sleepless, sarcastic or physically ill. And you can hold it in until it freezes and becomes depression or surfaces as an explosion much greater than the real or imagined hurt. Or, you can acknowledge the irritation, frustration or hurt as soon as possible.

1. Remember - you are what you say, what you do, what you think and what you feel. Your feelings are as individual as your footprints. No person is responsible for them but you.
2. Anger usually follows another feeling – such as frustration, fear or hurt - which went by unrecognised. Learn to notice the other feelings first.
3. To be hurt or afraid or frustrated are to be human. Try to express your feelings in words.
4. Accept anger as one way people get what they want. It's not the only way and certainly not the best way. What you achieve with a temper tantrum is control over another person, not cooperation.
5. Try to see people in a different light. Instead of assuming that they're behaving in certain ways to hurt or anger you, realise that sometimes it's the only way they know how to react in a stressful situation.
6. When you're around someone being angry, try listening not to the other's angry words, but to the feelings behind the words. What do you hear? Stress? Pain?
7. The way in which you become angry and what you do about such feelings are both habits. If you regularly let off steam by yelling at someone else, throwing a plate or hitting your child,

see it for what it is: a habit which can be unlearned if you choose to change it. In some cases, the unlearning may require the help of a professional.
8. Physical exercise relieves tension. It can help reduce the strain of a bad day at work or a quarrel with your spouse. But it's never the whole answer.
9. Saving up minor irritations for one big argument will not provide as much healthy relief as dealing with them, one at a time, as they occur.
10. After becoming angry, don't 'drive around for a while to cool off.' Walk around or run around or talk it out but avoid using machinery of any kind. The automobile may seem to be a convenient, anonymous escape hatch. For the angry driver, it's a hazard to his own safety and to the well-being of those around him.

'Take a closer look at how you handle life's ups and downs.'

Angry feelings are harmful when they're totally unexpressed or when they're expressed through physical violence to a child or another adult. If anger is more of a problem than you can handle alone, get professional help.

How do you handle anger?

To determine how well you handle anger, answer the following questions with:

   1 = yes

   2 = no

   3 = sometimes

1. Do I usually walk away from the other person when I'm angry?
2. Do I usually keep quiet when I'm angry [silent treatment?]
3. Do I simmer for days and then vent my anger in a big blow-up?
4. Do I appear to feel hurt when I'm actually angry? [Want sympathy?]
5. Do I take out my anger on someone other than the person at whom I'm angry?
6. Do I express my anger by labelling the other person rather than dealing with their behaviour?
7. When someone else is angry with me, do I have problems keeping my composure without blustering?

8. Do I have trouble 'Keeping My Cool' when accused of something I didn't do and retaliate verbally?
9. Do I feel hurt and withdraw when someone is angry with me rather than facing the issue openly with that person?

Rating:

Answers 1 = yes: Require work

Answers 2 = no : No problems here

Answers 3 = Sometimes: [Judge for yourself whether these are causing you problems. If so, work on solving them.]

Dealing with my Own Anger:

Here's another questionnaire. Circle the applicable answer:

1. When I'm angry, I usually feel:
   a) Afraid to say anything directly, because I don't want to hurt the other person's feelings.
   b) Afraid that if I *do* say something, it will sound aggressive, and others won't like me.
   c) Okay about expressing what's on my mind.
   d) Anxious and confused about what I want to say.
2. When I'm angry with someone, I usually:
   a) Drop hints about my feelings, hoping s/he will get the message.
   b) Tell the person in a direct way, what I want and feel okay about it.
   c) Avoid the person for a while, while I calm down and the anger wears off.
   d) Blow up and tell him/her off.
   e) Express my anger sarcastically – getting my point across with some humour or a dig.
3. If I'm angry with someone, I usually:
   a) Give hints about how I'm feeling, hoping s/he will get the message.
   b) Blow up and tell person off.
   c) Be sarcastic - get my point across with humour or a dig.
   d) Tell them how I feel and feel good about it.
   e) Avoid the person until I calm down.
4. When I'm angry, I usually:
   a) Feel anxious and don't know what I want to say.
   b) Feel comfortable about saying what's on my mind.

c) Don't say anything, because I don't want to hurt the other person's feelings.
d) If I do say something, it'll sound aggressive, and others won't like me.

Dealing with Others' Anger:

5. When someone gets angry with me, I usually:
   a) Think s/he doesn't like me.
   b) Feel too scared to ask why.
   c) Feel confused and upset.
   d) Think I have a right to understand why s/he is angry and to respond to it.
   e) Immediately feel wronged.
   f) Feel guilty.
6. When someone gets angry with me, what I usually do is:
   a) End up blustering.
   b) Back off.
   c) Ask him/her to explain his/her anger further or else I respond to it in some other equally straightforward manner.
   d) Get angry in return.
   e) Apologise if I don't understand why s/he's angry.
   f) Try to smooth it over.
   g) Make a joke out of it and try to get him/her to forget the flare-up.
   h) Give him/her the 'silent treatment.'

Rate Yourself:

The following answers identify assertive beliefs and behaviours:

1. (c) 2. (b) & (c) 3. (d) 4. (b) 5. (d) 6. (c)

Repression of anger:

Since childhood, women, more often men, are trained to hold back and control their negative feelings. This kind of conditioning results in two types of people who:

1. Hold in Resentment:

For whatever reasons, they've never learned to express their anger. No matter what the provocation, they clench their teeth and hold in their resentment. In some cases, they aren't even aware they're angry. They often have physical problems [psychosomatic illnesses.]

2. Don't Express Anger Properly:

They too haven't learned to express their anger appropriately. Instead of showing displeasure over the minor, irritating day-to-day episodes, they say nothing at the time. Then, a chance remark triggers a red flash of rage, and they lash out in violent anger. This fury has unfortunate consequences: The person feels terrible, and they alienate others.

Both are extremes. These individuals haven't learned how to express their feelings effectively when someone interferes with their rights, places obstacle in their path or violates their dignity. Uncontrolled lashing out is not a positive expression of anger.

Many believe [incorrectly] that anger is always a dangerous, powerful emotion. If they get really angry, they'll lose somebody's love, provoke anger in return or people won't like them. They've got this backwards. It's the repression of anger - not its expression - that's dangerous. Besides it doesn't matter a bit whether everyone likes them - that's an impossible goal, one that's guaranteed to frustrate them. People won't like them any more if they never get mad - in fact, they may like them even less for it.

Here are some of the effects of repressed anger:

Depression:

Depression is an illness caused by measurable changes in brain chemistry. It's more common in younger people, but the elderly also suffer. Normally, some important loss triggers depression. Younger people feel despondent when they lose items of value, friends, health, promotions, income and value as a human being. As people age, they lose many items of value - jobs, income, prestige, friends and health. For most people, recovery follows a period of grief or serious loss, but for others depression follows.

In the elderly, the most common signs of depression are insomnia, loss of interest in usual activities and loss of energy. Often there is weight loss as well. Difficulty concentrating, feelings of worthlessness and thoughts of suicide round out the picture. The person may sit around all day or become unusually active, although this latter response is uncommon.

The problem is that these symptoms may lead doctors to worry about Alzheimer's disease [in the elderly] cancer or some other illness, rather than depression. It's common that depression accompanies other illnesses. There are three important reasons to recognise and treat depression.

First, suicide is extremely common. Depression can be anger they're turning against themselves because they feel so helpless about the situation. The resulting depression can become so severe that they think of suicide. Some even carry out the thought. In most cases it's preventable, but we need to look hard for its warning signs.

Second, people with depression suffer. Quality of life is poor and they're unable to be enthusiastic or enjoy activities. Depressed people might say they 'don't feel right' or, 'don't feel at all like themselves.' Prompt treatment makes most people feel better.

Third, identifying depression often can clarify what's wrong for an elderly person who complains about an unending series of physical complaints. This can be of big relief to the physician and can save the patient the expense and risk of diagnostic tests.

Entire books are written about the drugs used to treat depression. The most important points though, are that these drugs can be extremely helpful and effective. Unfortunately, they also may have some dangerous side effects.

There's solid evidence that the very best treatment for depression is a combination of carefully used anti-depressant medication and counselling.

Transference of Anger:

Unable to face what they're really angry about, some shift it to another cause. i.e.: something goes wrong at a party. They say nothing, but later blame their spouse for something minor s/he did.

Long battles:

These often don't concern what the person's really angry about. They occur because they've shifted their goal, from sharing, to feelings of hurting the other person. They forget where they want to go. Their anger takes over and they can't stop themselves.

Temper Tantrums:

As shown in Chapter 6, this is a form of indirect aggression, in the form of childish, inappropriate, uncontrolled expression of anger [which anything can trigger.] This could be some trivial current happening or something that took place long ago that they may have stewed about for years.

Psychosomatic Illnesses:

Repression of anger can cause many physical illnesses. Some of these are tension headaches, stiff muscles, insomnia, over- or under-eating, migraines, ulcers and heart attacks.

Techniques to handle anger:

Anger is a very real part of everyone. The time has come for us to accept that we have a right to it and learn to express it. Here are some ideas that work:

Keep your cool:

Keeping your cool under fire takes concentrated effort. If you're quick to become angry, focus your energies on stopping your automatic responses. Try the following tactics:

Tune into your feelings.

- Narrow down what caused your anger.
- Try to understand why you got angry [fear etc.]
- Deal with your anger realistically; by sharing feelings with the person who upset you. Communicate - don't shut them out.
- Take a walk. Use adrenalin effectively, toward constructive activities.

1. Don't rationalise your reasons for not expressing anger.

Don't pay attention to such things as, *'I'm afraid to say anything because I'll hurt the other person's feelings.'* These are ways of explaining to yourself why you don't do what you've never learned to do. Instead of dwelling on the reasons you don't express anger, concentrate on learning how to do it.

2. Try to correct the behaviour of the person causing the anger.

Don't attack the person.

3. Target your angry behaviour.

a. How do you express anger?

- Do you show too little?
- Do you come on too strong, too weak, or not at all?

- Do you express anger days, months, even years after the provoking incident?
- Is your nonverbal communication of anger appropriate?
- Do you fall into the trap of attributing your anger to someone else ('*You* make me angry')?
- Do you mouth angry words, but say them in a whisper that the other person can barely hear?
- Do you slouch or keep your eyes on the floor as you say them?

You *own* your responses. Your ability to make choices about your emotions puts responsibility for what you are and how you feel - on you. When you express anger, you should try to relate your comments to what the other person has done. Say, *'I'm angry because you always leave the newspaper on the floor.'*

(b) The different situations in which you have difficulty.

- Is it at work? If so, break it down. Does your anger have to do with co-workers, subordinates or superiors?
- In impersonal situations? Some people always show their anger towards taxi drivers and others who can't express annoyance back to them. This is very unfair.
- Friends and acquaintances? With some people the more distant the acquaintance is, the easier they find it to express anger. With others it's the reverse. The closer the friend, the easier it is to say, *'I'm furious.'*
- There are some people who feel that the only time they're being honest is when they express anger.
- Social Situations? Can you get angry in a group conversation but not one-on-one? Do you feel safer in a group - or the reverse?
- In close relationships? Some can express anger only to a spouse. When asked, *'Why?'* the answer is often, *'S/he's the only one in the world who wouldn't leave me if I show anger.'*
- Time of the day? Do you become angry more often at night or in the morning? What day of the week or season of the year is the worst for you?

4. Recognise that you have a right to feel anger and express it.

Anger doesn't have to lead to violence. If you have doubts about your right to be angry, perhaps you've done something *you* don't like. Maybe you feel like yelling at yourself and instead, take it out on another person.

5. Avoid direct expression of anger.

Perhaps you sit and sulk - seething inside - but refuse to say why you're angry. Or you communicate hurt instead of anger *'You shouldn't have done this to me'* Or you use sarcasm to express anger, making it difficult for the other person to cope with the situation. They know something's wrong, but the sarcasm pushes them away and they can't pin down just what's bothering you. Be clear and direct in your communication with others.

6. Express your anger when you feel it.

In this way, you can frequently avoid unpleasant consequences. Otherwise, you may lash out at the wrong person, for the wrong reasons.

7. Don't make the mistake of not going far enough in your anger.

Some people make tentative stabs at expressing their anger - then abort it. Don't just mention that you're angry; find a solution to the problem or situation that caused the anger.

8. Realise that you have the right to raise your voice.

It's perfectly all right to pound the table, swear or shout, as long as you're not intimidating or taking advantage of another! Expressing anger involves more than just a higher voice level, it's the words you use, body position and movement. Some treat anger with silence or place distance emotionally between themselves and the person causing the anger. This is using indirect aggression - an extremely unfair tactic to get your way. It's better to talk about and resolve the underlying problem or it will resurface again later.

9. Practice your new skills in a safe environment:

- Role-play the situation with someone you trust. Monitor yourself, your level of anger on a scale of 1 to 10.

- Determine ways you could have handled your anger better than you did at the actual time of the anger.
- If you have trouble venting your anger on someone close to you, write down all the situations that make you furious with him or her. Ask him or her to do the same and regularly make appointments to get together. Don't dump on each other - just discuss the important items on your respective lists. Make a vow to each other that you *will* listen and try hard to understand each other's position - one talks; one listens.
- If your anger brings about tension and interferes with things you do, get it out of your system with physical exercise [not competitive sports!] This works when can't express anger - for instance, the other person is out of town.
- In your bedroom, hit your pillow for two minutes; curse into the pillow - release your anger.
- Grab your racquetball racquet, draw the face of the person you're mad at on a ball and smash it into the wall.

10. Make the deliberate decision not to express anger.

Initially, expressing anger may make you feel important. There are times, though when you cannot express your anger. For example, when a frail older person angers you or they can't handle your anger health-wise or if the child is too young to reason with.

11. Remember, your choice is not limited to expressing anger or not expressing it.

Sometimes you can use a supportive approach. For example: Your supervisor yells at you and commands you to do something you consider completely unprofessional. Count to ten and say, *'Is there something wrong Mr. Bailey? I know there must be or you would never speak to me that way.'*

Most feelings of anger stem from too much pressure and stress. Relieving your stress level will help you with handling everyday pressures. Can you handle all situations relating to anger every time? Probably not - you're human. But, if you can control even five percent more of the situations you face, you've improved your lot in life.

12. Therapeutic touching.

As a child, do you remember when your mother 'kissed it better?' Do you remember the hugs and cuddles you received after you were lost in a department store, and they finally found you? Did it usually have the desired affect? It probably did. These acts are therapeutic touching. A compassionate touch, often known as laying on of hands, can be a powerful curative.

Touching is an almost essential nutrient to all humans. As adults, we may feel an impulse to hug someone when s/he has experienced a loss, but we don't do so in less extreme circumstances. We've been so alienated in our society from touching people, that touching others becomes restricted to close family members or in sexual relations.

Therapeutic touching allows your heart rate and blood pressure to go down. Your breathing becomes regular, and your muscle tension decreases. The same is true whether you're the 'toucher' or the 'touchee.' The next time you have a headache - before reaching for a painkiller ask someone to give you a neck rub. If you don't have a human handy, stroking a dog or cat can have much the same effect.

Human contact is a factor in healing. Emotionally satisfying friendships, close family ties, are more potent in curing than many of medical science's drugs and treatment. Those who are alienated from family and friends, have double the chance of becoming sick. Men and women trapped in unhappy marriages are likely to suffer ill health. People who're happy with their relationships have better immune systems. Good friends are good medicine.

We've heard that confession is good for the soul. Having an empathetic friend who's willing to listen, can have a profound effect on how we feel about ourselves.

If you choose to be a good friend to someone else, you also might gain some unexpected benefits. Doing volunteer work results in the release of endorphins, the body's natural opiates. The health benefits include relief from stress-related conditions such as headaches and backaches and the emotional payback of a feeling of self-worth.

There's a form of 'bad helping.' Some find themselves in extremely demanding or depressing situations where they feel helpless or out of control. For example, those who help the homeless sometimes don't see much gain because of their efforts. This could increase their stress, rather than relieve it. The answer is to find some other form of volunteer work that makes you feel good.

13. Meditation:

Quiet contemplation and meditation can do wonders to those suffering the effects of living in a stressed-out or angry society. Spending fifteen to twenty minutes a day quietly meditating can change your life. You'll benefit by achieving harmony in your body and emotions that can result in the feeling of having more control over your body.

One woman found that she could control her migraine headaches; another could use breathing methods to control her motion sickness. It also gives your brain a much-needed rest from the rush-rush-rush of society. You'll become refreshed and ready to tackle the world.

Heal thyself

We've long known that there's a co-relation between mind and body. We've heard stories about miraculous events such as the 110-pound woman who lifted a two-ton car off her trapped child and the football star that played an entire game with a broken shinbone. Medical authorities are beginning to see the co-relationship between state of mind and what the body can and cannot do.

There's a definite link between a healthy personality, an optimistic attitude, and a vigorous immune system. If each of us decides to be in control, keep cheerful and relaxed, we'll give ourselves an optimum chance of becoming and staying well physically, emotionally, and mentally.

CHAPTER TEN

TURNING THINGS AROUND

'Happiness is not having what you want.
It's wanting what you have!'

Using Your Abilities

Most people use only about five to twenty percent of their full capabilities and talents in a lifetime. How do you know you couldn't be a concert pianist, if you've never tried to play a piano? How do you know whether you could be one of the world's finest gourmet cooks, if you've never tried to cook? How do you know if you could be an excellent computer programmer, if you've never used one? What percentage of your abilities do you think *you* use? What could you have been good at, but haven't tried?

People usually try to fit into the mould society says they should - to forget their own uniqueness. When they're children, they're expected to fit a mould [become a clone.] They must live up to parental expectations and are programmed to please others first. In doing this, they find themselves being educated and specialising in occupations they haven't chosen themselves. They end up in jobs that don't interest them and spend their lives doing work they hate.

Some people are very comfortable being 'one of the crowd,' and there's nothing wrong with that. There *is* something wrong though, if they suffer from depression or regularly must suppress frustration and anger. If they've stopped risk-taking into areas beyond their normal everyday activities, it's hard breaking out of their 'rut.'

Early conditioning may raise barricades that stop them from using their imagination and creativity. Others give them the impression that to make a mistake is a 'sin.' Unfortunately, the belief that making mistakes is wrong can result in tunnel-vision. They believe that if they take risks, they might get burned. A mistake is just that; a mistake - nothing more - nothing less. They should throw away any guilt feelings they might feel and learn from their mistakes instead.

One way you can identify new activities you might try, is to list the activities you now do well. What activities could you be doing that are similar and therefore you stand a good chance of succeeding at?

Your choice doesn't have to be sports related; it could be occupation related. Those who have banking experience may excel at accounting, financial management or be an investment broker. These occupations have the common thread - dealing with figures. If you have a 'gift of the gab,' you could enhance those qualities by joining Toastmasters. Then you could try for a sales position or work on the executive of organisations where these skills are definite assets.

Use the exceptional skills you were born with. Unfortunately, you'll never know what they are, unless you test them. A happy person is not necessarily from a certain background or has particular attributes. Rather, s/he is a person with a certain set of attitudes, skills, and abilities. S/he isn't afraid of going out on a limb - that's where the fruit is!

How about the activities you think you're not very good at? Have you tried these activities lately? If you're not good at sports - when was the last time you tried one? Or do you feel the test you gave them at the awkward age of thirteen was test enough? We often let failures we have as children to unreasonably influence our entire lives.

Analyse yourself. Do you have any negative tapes running around in your brain that may be stopping you from trying something new? Test your abilities. You certainly aren't the same person you were when someone placed the original negative tapes in your subconscious.

Taking risks

Webster's Dictionary defines the word RISK: *'To expose to the chance of injury, damage or loss.'*

To some, taking a risk of any kind brings forward the following thoughts:

To laugh is to risk appearing a fool.
To weep is to risk appearing sentimental.
To reach out to another, is to risk involvement.
To expose feelings, is to risk exposing your true self.

To place your ideas and your dreams before the crowd is to risk their loss.
To love is to risk not being loved in return.
To live is to risk dying.
To hope is to risk despair.
To try is to risk failure.

People who risk nothing do nothing - have nothing - are nothing. They may avoid suffering and sorrow, but they simply cannot learn, feel, change, grow, love or live - chained by their beliefs. They're slaves who forfeit their freedom. We must take risks, because the greatest hazard in life is to risk nothing. Only those who risk, are free.

Risk-takers are spontaneous. Spontaneity is being able to try anything on the spur of the moment, just because you think it will be something you'd enjoy. It means you eliminate any pre-judgment. Are you spontaneous? Or do you always eat the same foods, wear the same kind of clothes, live in the same neighbourhood, reject others who are 'different,' reject new ideas before testing them, work at the same type of job, have vacations at the same place and keep the same friends?

Others insist on security in external items such as possessions, money, houses, cars, jobs or position in the community. Take these possessions away from some and they can't function. These people blame external forces for the negative situations that happen to them in life, rather than what is internal in themselves.

Do you over- or under-emphasise the results of everything you do? Have you hurt others in the past by acting too soon, with too little information? Analyse what your actions do to others and how it will affect other projects and you'll be less likely to make a mistake again.

Those who take command of their future have the unshakable knowledge that they can overcome anything - if they set their minds to it. With enough self-motivation and effort, they know they can be anything they choose. This force is internal and external forces seldom affect it. It sets the foundation for everything the person does in life.

You need courage to take risks, but life without risk is very mundane and boring. All progress involves flying in the face of the old way versus a new way. Too many people equate the unknown with danger. Some fear not being able to 'pull it off,' that they'll fail. Their programming leads them to believe that failure's bad, so in taking risks, they face the chance of ending up with not one, but two bad feelings. They feel they've failed at what they tried to do, with the added extra burden of lowered self-esteem. If you wait until 'you're in the mood,' you may wait an eternity before reaching your goals.

Some personalities thrive on risk-taking and love living 'on the edge.' They're likely to have an immense influence on society. These people explore new areas and occasionally break the rules. Men more than women [who are conditioned **not** to do these things] are more likely to be the ones who parasail, SCUBA dive and skydive. They take charge of their own destinies and appear to choose employment that offers variety, excitement and an opportunity to use all their talents and abilities. Most in this group make excellent entrepreneurs, because they're less likely to fear failure.

Mature people are less willing to take risks than young adults. By middle age most people have a large number of activities they have no intention of doing again, because they've tried them once and failed. This prevents future exploration and experimentation to find solutions about why it didn't work the first time.

What can we do about this lowered self-esteem? We can learn to use our abilities to their fullest. You can probably remember when an employer turned you down for a promotion or job or you lost a game and felt terrible about it. Can you honestly look back and say that you used your full capabilities? Could you have given more effort towards getting the job or winning the game?

Race horses sometimes win only 'by a nose.' Why do we assume that we can't just win 'by a nose' at what we attempt? We really don't have to be that much better than everyone else - just a nose better. To expect otherwise, would mean we're expecting ourselves to be superhuman.

I always approach new ideas with an open mind. When approaching a new task, I rationalise, *'I've never tried this before - but I'll try my best.'* I don't panic if I don't do something well [and know I've given my best try.] Instead, I acknowledge that this is something I don't do very well and try something else. If I *do* succeed, the positive results usually spur me on to try other new adventures. The momentum of my success keeps me 'up.' With this positive approach, I find that three out of five things I try, I succeed at and the ratio is improving.

Do you let yourself feel that you've failed at something, when you've given it your best try? Early in my life, a wise friend advised me to take the word 'failure' out of my vocabulary. I was to tell myself that I just hadn't succeeded at something. I made it a learning experience, rather than expecting myself to be perfect. I learned that I couldn't be good at everything! If I thought I had to be, I'd be bound to spend most of my life in misery.

To begin your risk-taking training, start with a task where you can almost guarantee success, then increase the level of risk accordingly. Stop expecting to fail. Learn that you can't expect to succeed every time.

Optimists handle stress better than pessimists because they emphasise the positive effects of a stressful situation. They see it as a learning experience. Optimists seek social support, such as asking family or friends for help. They look for ways they can improve their failures. They identify those that were beyond their control, and they couldn't influence anyway.

Pessimists forget the experience, believing that they couldn't do anything to change or improve the situation. They repeatedly continue making the same mistakes.

How can I improve my risk-taking?

If you're holding off doing something because you're afraid to take the risk, do the following:

a) Define as closely as possible, what you think the risk is.
b) Determine what you could *gain* emotionally and physically by trying it.
c) Determine what you could *lose* emotionally and physically by trying it.
d) Do you need more information before taking the risk? Where would you get this information? Who has this kind of information?
e) What's the *best* thing that could happen if you took the chance and tried it?
f) What's the *worst* thing that could happen if you took the chance and tried it?

g) How could you lessen the risk?
h) Is it now worth taking the risk?

How you appear to others

Although people know what's attractive in someone else, they often don't see what's attractive in themselves. I'm sure you've heard the expression, 'Beauty is in the eyes of the beholder.' It's true, for appearance is very much a question of individuality or what we bring to it and of how we perceive others. For instance, have you ever found yourself commenting on how good looking a friend of yours was. Later you realised that it really wasn't his physical attractiveness you were referring to, but that friend's warmth, his goodness, his smile, and his helpful personality?

If you thought some more about it, you might even admit that perhaps this attractive friend was less than picture-book perfect. But then, it isn't a perfect profile or a particular feature that makes any person attractive, is it?

Believing in yourself and your abilities has a great deal to do with projecting a positive, attractive image to others in your world. It really isn't a question of being blonde, brunette or being thin, of being brown- or blue-eyed. Instead, it's whether or not you have an open smile, an essence that shows sincerity towards others and a facial expression that's pleasant and positive. These are the real assets that make a person appealing and attractive. Just think of a good-looking face that's always pouting or looking angry and you'll realise, no one wants to look at it.

If you have good health, if you make the most of what you were born with, if you've learned how to accent your positive features and play down the negative ones, you'll be working towards the elusive goal of good looks. For clearly, there is a prejudice within our society towards good looks. So why not be the best possible you, you can be? That's what good looks is all about!

How long does it take you to size up others? Five, ten minutes or even less? Surveys show that what an employment interviewer sees in the first four minutes of an interview decides whether they will hire you or not. This is before they even ask about your qualifications! What are they using to determine their opinion of you?

Your appearance.

Your appearance is extremely important to your feelings of self-confidence as well as your impressions on others.

'You never have a second chance to make a first impression.'

Good grooming is a must. If you look good - you usually feel good. This doesn't only mean dressing well, but cleanliness both in your dress and personal grooming. Many people create a negative impression on others because of the following. See if you need to improve on any of these areas:

a. Too much or too little perfume, aftershave, or cologne?
b. Body odour from lack of bathing or wearing clothing for more than one day?
c. Improper hairstyle or cut?
d. Men who are not clean-shaven, moustache or beard is scruffy?
e. Women not making the most of themselves with makeup, either too much or too little?
f. Female office workers with runs in pantyhose.
g. Wearing badly outdated or unsuitable style of clothing.
h. Un-coordinated outfits or poor colour sense of what goes together.
i. Dirty, spotted, or wrinkled clothing.

Another self-esteem booster can be the use of colour. Because I'm a seminar leader, I always must look positive. Occasionally, I have a 'blah' day and don't feel up to par. I find that on those days my inclination is to wear drab colours. I've found that if I wear more cheerful colours, I feel more cheerful [and fool other people into thinking I feel better than I do.]

One man came to me for career counselling. He'd been working as a project engineer and normally worked on-site, so naturally wore construction clothing. He was having physical problems from working in adverse weather conditions and wished to find an indoor position of some sort. I helped him put together a resume and he applied for several related engineering jobs that did not require him to work on-site.

His problems occurred when it was time to change his image. He admitted that he didn't have many suits so would have to buy a new wardrobe. His problem was that he didn't know what colours or styles to buy. I introduced him to an acquaintance who colour draped him and accompanied him when he made his purchases.

Before he headed out to his most important interview, he came to see me for a 'pep' talk. I couldn't believe the change in his appearance. When I had seen him in the past, he had worn earth-tone colours. Colour draping showed that they were not the right colours for his skin and hair colouring. He wore a blue-grey suit [with complementary shirt, tie, socks, and shoes] that set off his grey hair to perfection. The image he gave was of a distinguished, mature man [which was the image he wished to portray.] I complimented him on his appearance and sent him on his way with my best wishes.

The next day he called with the jubilant information that they had chosen him for the job. Not only did he look better in the colours that suited him, but he felt better too. Now, before he buys anything to add to his wardrobe, he checks his colour chart. That way, no matter what he takes out of his closet, the colour suits him.

If you haven't been colour-draped, you're probably wasting hundreds of dollars a year. Look in your closet and see how many items you've bought, that are still sitting on their hangers, because they 'just don't feel right.'

Ability to Communicate

Verbal fluency is one of the best communication skills a person can have. When you think of it - you're going to be speaking the rest of your life. If you can't say what you want to say, it's time to get help. Taking public speaking courses, belonging to Toastmasters and Toastmistress speaking clubs will help you learn this skill.

If you need to make presentations to others, the three secrets to success in public speaking are:

> ** Be sincere*
>
> ** Be brief*
>
> ** Be seated*

In addition, to saying what you want, you need to feel assertive enough to express your point of view. If you aren't sure of what you want to say, it will show in your speaking style. Watch that you don't become repetitive or jump from topic to topic and lose your audience. Many need to practice projecting their voices from their diaphragm.

Unfortunately, when public speaking, women have bad habits that are hard to break. Women use different body language and words than their male counterparts when making presentations to groups. When women are nervous, their voices can become shrill or appear breathless. This is because women hunch over when they're nervous. They use only the top part of their lungs to project their voices. They need to put their shoulders back to increase the volume of their chests so they can project their voices.

When making public presentations women's body language gives away their nervousness. They appear to take up as little space as possible [they tuck in all their ends.] Their shoulders and even their elbows look rigid. In some, their hands flutter to their faces when they're not sure of the point they're making. What their bodies and facial expressions ask for is approval - the raising of their eyebrows, head down and leaning forward. What their whole body implies is, 'Do you like what I'm saying?'

They often end sentences with a question such as, *'Don't you think this would be a good idea?'* They appear to need the approval of their audiences. Many of their statements end with their voices raised, as if they were asking a question. Unfortunately, this gives a very negative impression because they appear emotional and indecisive.

Women use words that are far more specific than those of men and use expressions such as, 'gorgeous, marvellous, superb and super.' They use the word 'so' too often - *'so beautiful,'* or, *'so extravagant.'* Women's speech is full of adjectives and qualifying phrases such as, 'I think ... I feel ... I guess ... or I believe ...'

Men on other hand say, 'uhm' more often. Men's voices deepen when they're nervous. Their posture often takes on a defensive stance when they're nervous, which expands their chests and gives their voices more volume.

If you're terrified about having to make a speech, try using a tape recorder to check your voice pattern or better yet, use a video camera to identify your failings. Use friends to critique your speeches. Practice, practice and practice some more, until you know you're going to do a good job. Self-confidence is one-half the battle when giving a presentation. The other half is preparation and factual information.

Non-verbal communication

We all have body language signals that match our personalities. We can identify a timid person by the way s/he acts or a depressed person by his or her dejected posture. We can identify the self-assured person by the way s/he walks, talks, dresses, and smiles.

Their posture, verbal fluency, tone or volume of voice and clarity of their comments are all rated. The confidence of their handshake, the gleam [or lack of it] in their eyes, their friendliness, poise and stability tell us far more than their words. We'll check their alertness, their general appearance and passive or aggressive behaviour. This could include watching for nervous tics, observing their energy level [are they hyperactive or lethargic.]

What does their personality tell us? Are they introverts or extroverts? What is their general attitude toward society? Are they leaders or followers? Are they organised or disorganised? Are they critical of others, buck-passers, swellheaded, over- or underweight?

We can identify those who are self-assured by the way they carry themselves. They sit with an open, receptive position, have a ready smile, have a gleam in their eye and are not afraid of showing their emotions and feelings.

If you feel overwhelmed by a situation, but want to make a good impression, you can change your self-image by acting. You can accomplish this by imitating the body language of a self-confident person. Continue this regularly. Eventually you'll feel more self-confident, and sure of yourself. Initially, you'll only be pretending and feel awkward at first, but if you keep at it, permanent changes are likely to appear. Only you can change your inner attitude towards yourself, feel good about yourself and become more self-assured.

Enthusiasm

Another ego booster is the use of enthusiasm. Enthusiasm, like positive thinking, is contagious. It's almost impossible to be exposed to enthusiasm for any length of time without catching some of it yourself. If you're going to be enthusiastic, you must first want to be enthusiastic. The first step is to participate in activities that interest you. The key to having interest is knowledge. Become even more interested in items you know the most about. Strangely, the more interested you become, the more you want to know. Knowledge, interest, knowledge, interest, knowledge, interest! It's a rolling stone that gathers more and more speed and this leads to enthusiasm.

I had the opportunity of asking the man who had hired me to do seminars for the University of Hawaii, what made him take a chance on me. He stated, *'You were so enthusiastic - I couldn't go wrong!'* This points out the need to 'run with ideas' as soon as you have them. I may have lost my enthusiasm, if I had waited until the next day to phone for the appointment. So, do it now!

Watch children at the zoo. What holds their interest more, the sleepy owl or the active seal? The moving, darting seals fascinated the children, and they almost ignored the sleepy owls. Which are you - an owl or a seal? The world will notice you if you're moving, animated, alive. Others will ignore you, if you sit lifeless like the owl. Remember, enthusiasm is contagious. Start the disease!

Energy level

People notice the kind of energy level you have. Just watching you walk will show them yours. If you shuffle along, they know you probably have a low energy level [at least at that moment.] If you bounce along, you probably have a high energy level.

Would you say you normally have a low, medium, or high energy level? If you said you normally have a low energy level, are you in a high stress, deadline-prone position? If so, you're probably under far more stress than you can comfortably handle. Try to find activities and positions that don't put you under this type of pressure.

It's also possible that your low energy level happens because, what you're doing makes you bored to tears. Assess your energy level when you're doing something you like to do? Is there any difference? If so, the signs point to finding a better position or change your lifestyle.

Those with a medium energy level can increase theirs by finding suitable employment. Use of effective time management helps too. If you find that life is nothing but hurry, hurry, hurry, you probably should take a time management class or read up on the topic, so you have less wasted time and energy.

Those blessed with a high energy level are lucky, but they should ask themselves whether they are spending their energy productively or non-productively. Some waste their energy on hyperactive behaviour. When high-energy people start channelling their energy in the right direction many become highly successful.

When we place high-energy people in routine positions with lots of leisure time, they'll eventually suffer from high stress levels. Put low-energy people in positions with constant deadlines and pressures and they'll suffer from high stress levels as well. Both people are in the wrong kind of lifestyle to suit their metabolisms.

You may notice that your energy levels change during the day. Some are morning people; some are best mid-afternoon, while others are night owls. Finding a job that enables you to work in your high-energy time can do wonders for your level of productivity.

Obtaining inner peace

When you feel you're in control of your life, you'll gain that elusive feeling of inner peace. Here are the steps you can take to help obtain this feeling:

1. Write down all your dreams. Many use a journal or daily diary to do this. Then set concrete goals to reach those dreams.
2. Seek and cultivate support groups. Keep in touch with this group - don't let your friendships lapse. Be fair in your exchanges with them - don't always take from them – give an equal measure of support in return. You may have to eliminate or lessen the time you spend with unsupportive friends.
3. Meditate or do something that's stress-reducing every day. Keep in tune with what your body's telling you about your stress level. Use stress relievers as soon as you notice you're in trouble. Avoid medications, drugs and alcohol to relieve your stress. Instead, depend on natural pleasures such as listening to your favourite music, going for a peaceful walk, reading a novel or whatever you find best to help you relieve your stress.
4. If you have limited time, take deep breaths to increase your oxygen level in your brain. Have a 'power nap' or a 'mental health break' where you mentally turn everything off for a set time.
5. Quit living in the past or the future. Concentrate on the now - this minute, this hour. Determine how you feel. If you're not feeling up to par, decide for yourself that you'll only give yourself a set number of minutes to continue feeling that way.

Then, after those minutes, tell yourself that you *are* going to feel better.

'Opportunity sometimes knocks very softly.'

Those who have attained inner peace say that they:

a) Are spontaneous and unafraid of trying new challenges.
b) Enjoy life and all it brings be it happiness or sadness.
c) Remember all their little successes and learn from their mistakes and failures.
d) Are more comfortable with negotiation than conflict.
e) Are in tune with others, use empathy to put themselves in the other person's place if s/he is upset or acting badly. They can stop and analyse why the person may be acting in such a negative way. This helps them keep control over their own responses instead of immediately defending themselves against the actions of others.
f) Know when to turn off worry. They analyse whether they have the power to change a situation or not. If they can do nothing personally about the problem, they turn it off and don't waste their valuable energy worrying about it. Instead, they concentrate their efforts on dealing with situations where they do have the power to change the situation.
g) Are proud of their achievements and expect to continue being proud of their expected future achievements. Onward and upward is their motto. Seldom are they upset by what others would call failure.
h) Have strong feelings of closeness with others that makes them want to be good towards others. They're thoughtful to others' needs and rights as well as their own. They realise that giving is a two-way street and enjoy the feeling of giving.
i) Obtain happiness from the little pleasures in life. They stop often to 'smell the flowers.' They take time out of their busy life to stop and enjoy the moment.
j) Make things happen, rather than wait for them to happen.

Don't worry - Be happy

This catchy song had everyone singing. Don't worry - be happy! Wouldn't life be great if we could do that? What steps can we take to help ourselves achieve that goal?

1. Analyse your worries. Worry motivates us to take necessary action. Most people worry, but some overdo it. Others react by

avoiding the situation and don't act. Worrying offers an illusion of control. Some believe if they worry enough, magically it will prevent the bad situation from happening. It's a form of burying their heads in the sand. These people are out of control of their lives. They wait for something to happen and seldom make things happen. Get cracking and do something about your worries, don't just let them fester and contaminate everything positive you try to do.

2. Don't let yourself get caught up in a catch-22 situation. Once negative thinking takes hold, the person's negative thoughts can quickly get out of hand. The mind is very imaginative and will think of all types of weird and frightening situations that could happen. For instance, the parents who are waiting for their teenager who's out after a mid-night curfew, visualises their child as:

   a) being in a car accident,
   b) being attacked by a mugger,
   c) has run away from home,
   d) is drinking and is ashamed to come home,

   When the child appears, the parents lash out in anger, because they realise their worry was for nothing. The next time the child is late, the same collage of worries will re-surface. Instead, the parent should be thinking ahead about what the teenager should be doing if s/he knows s/he is going to be late in the future. Instead of yelling at the teenager, they should be explaining the fears they had and explain what they expect the teenager to do next time they have to be late. The parent also should identify the consequences should the event recur.

3. Recognise that the worry you're feeling can cause serious hazards to your health. The stress involved is probably playing havoc with you both physically and mentally. Know that it's important that you keep your stress to tolerable levels. Over fifty percent of the reasons people visit their doctor are because of stress and excessive anxiety. The key lies in recognising the worry for what it is and letting the thought slip away which is not always easy to do.

4. Spend some time daily to mull over problems you're facing. Give yourself only a set time to do this but be willing to spend more time on it if you're on a problem-solving roll. During that

time, solve as many of the problems you're worrying about as possible. This way, you'll confine worry to a specific time that will allow you to 'turn off' your worries after you've dealt with them.

5. Recognise when you're beginning to worry. Worrying sneaks up on us, so it's important to be sensitive to our thought patterns. Tell yourself that you'll spend adequate time dealing with it at your 'worry time.' Then remove it from your mind.

Here's another method you can try to eliminate much of your worry:

a) Write down situations that cause you frustration, worry or anger. (This is in your personal life, your business life and your social life).
b) Determine whether:
   i. You have the power to change the situation or
   ii. You don't have the power to change the situation.
c) If you don't have the power to change the situation, why are you wasting your valuable time worrying about it?
d) If you do have the power to change the situation, what do you intend to do about it? Or are you just going to whine and complain about it?

Sometimes we forget that we aren't practising up for the 'real thing.' This is the only time we're at this point in life. Living for today and having a positive attitude towards tomorrow, will help us enjoy the time we have.

CHAPTER ELEVEN

How To Be A Winner

'Success is to get what you want.
Luck is to keep what you get.'

Success

Everyone has their personal definition of what success means to them. What would it take to make you feel successful? What does the word 'success' mean to you? I feel successful when I set goals and achieve them. To some it's having enough money. To others it is good health, happiness, loving family that's turning out well, good friends, recognition from their peers.

Some believe that they must be born with a 'success personality,' or a winning combination of qualities that ensures success. Most successful people have achieved in a given field. They have channelled their energies towards being the best they can be in their chosen area of endeavour. These people share many similar personality traits. The major one is their ability to call on their common sense, when faced with something they've never dealt with before.

In addition to being experts in their chosen field of endeavour, they have enough confidence in themselves that they pick themselves up if they didn't achieve the level, they were expecting. They learn from their mistakes. Most have average to high intelligence levels and know how to get things done. They're the goal setters and are spurred on to greater heights as they reach their goals.

Medical experts say that the reason people become tired, is not because they do too much - but rather because they do too little! By just giving more effort and working a little bit harder, you can't help but get greater results. Whether you want health, happiness, more money or whatever, it's not going to come to you, just because you want it.

People who work the longest hours with the most satisfaction are often the self-employed. Why not try the same approach yourself? No - I don't mean starting your own business, but why not look at your job the same way as a person who owns his or her own business? Pretend you're working for yourself and ultimately, you'll be the benefactor of your efforts.

'Success is getting up just one more time than you fall down.'

People read books, go to meetings, take courses, attend conventions and probe frantically in all directions for new secrets and methods for achieving success. But somehow, they almost deliberately avoid admitting the answer was right before them. They appear to be unwilling to admit that simple, good, old-fashioned hard work can be the basis of success. Success is almost always preceded by hard work.

How do winners differ from losers?

Is one of your goals to be a winner? Here are some behaviours of consistent winners. They:

- ✓ Are positive thinkers who use visualisation to help them reach their goals in life.
- ✓ Like virtually everything about life. They're enthusiastic about life and want all they can get out of it.
- ✓ Are seldom sick - treat their bodies well by eating and exercising properly.
- ✓ Have a high energy level - require less sleep than the average person.
- ✓ Show you they're proud of themselves by their clothing, appearance, posture and even the gleam in their eyes.
- ✓ Are comfortable doing just about anything - are spontaneous and flexible.
- ✓ Are creative, imaginative - are seldom bored.
- ✓ Are empathetic - have insight into the behaviour of others.
- ✓ Want to be a winner on their own rather than being a success through the weaknesses or bad performance of others.
- ✓ Get their self-esteem, personal value and worth from inside. External forces have little effect on them.
- ✓ Associate with other winners. They don't equate being successful in ventures with their own level of self-worth.
- ✓ Don't waste time complaining, grumbling, whining or feeling sorry for themselves.
- ✓ Pursue activities they're good at or win at.
- ✓ Are free of guilt feelings.

- ✓ Learn from their mistakes.
- ✓ Are organised - good time managers.
- ✓ Are direct in their interaction with others - don't use manipulation to get their way.
- ✓ Are honest - don't pass-the-buck or blame others.
- ✓ Know when others are trying to manipulate them.
- ✓ Understand that mistakes are just that - mistakes.
- ✓ Live in the present, not the past or the future.
- ✓ Lack fear of the unknown, are doers rather than watchers.
- ✓ Have and enjoy good humour - laugh with people not at them.
- ✓ Are independent thinkers and act accordingly.
- ✓ Are selective about love but love deeply and sensitively in close relationships. Their partners in life also must be independent.
- ✓ Don't seek or expect approval from others.
- ✓ Are almost blunt in their honesty.
- ✓ Dislike small talk and cocktail parties. Their conversations are deep and like privacy and enjoy their own company.
- ✓ Know when they're on a roll and they run with it.
- ✓ Grab new situations as they appear.
- ✓ Know that doing their best is more important than being the best.

How to tell a winner from a loser

A winner says, *'Let's find out.'*
A loser says, *'Nobody knows.'*

When a winner makes a mistake, s/he says, *'I was wrong.'*
When a loser makes a mistake, s/he says, *'It wasn't my fault.'*

A winner isn't nearly as afraid of losing as
A loser is secretly afraid of winning.

A winner paces him- or herself.
A loser has only two speeds - hysterical and lethargic.

A winner works harder than a loser and has more time.
A loser is always 'too busy' to do what is necessary.
A winner goes through a problem.
A loser goes around it and never gets past it.

A winner makes commitments.
A loser makes promises.

A winner says, *'I'm good, but not as good as I ought to be.'*
A loser says, *'I'm not as bad as a lot of other people.'*

A winner tries to learn from those who are superior to him or her.
A loser tries to tear down those who are superior to him or her.

A winner explains.
A loser explains away.

A winner feels responsible for more than his or her job.
A loser says, *'I only work here.'*

A winner says, *'There ought to be a better way to do it.'*
A loser says, *'That's the way it's always been done here.'*

'If it's to be - it's up to me.'

Putting it all together

- ✓ Don't blame others for your self-esteem level and expect external happenings to change your life. Make things happen yourself.
- ✓ Don't wait for 'big brother' or your employer to 'see' your talents. [You may be overlooked]. Make sure they know where you want to go and how you intend to help yourself get there [through education and training.]
- ✓ If you need training to do your job properly - get it.
- ✓ If you're stuck in a negative type of lifestyle, take action *now*, today, to do something to better your life.
- ✓ Make every effort to think of yourself in a favourable light - become your best friend and treat yourself accordingly.
- ✓ Eliminate your fear of failure by taking calculated, reasonable risks.
- ✓ Be flexible - bend with the wind to adapt to new situations.
- ✓ Don't be sensitive to criticism - realise that making mistakes is okay as long as you learn from them.
- ✓ Eliminate any fears you may have related to success.
- ✓ Don't 'should on yourself,' or say, 'if only,' or start every second sentence with the word 'but' [and give reasons why something won't work.] Instead concentrate on the positives.
- ✓ Stop being a fence-sitter [you just get slivers.] If a task needs to be done, or a decision needs to be made - do it!

- ✓ Don't be dependent on others mentally, physically, and especially emotionally.
- ✓ Say *'no'* when it's appropriate.
- ✓ Forgive those that have trespassed against you, otherwise you'll remain tied to them and their actions emotionally.
- ✓ Set specific life and career goals for yourself.
- ✓ Obtain career counselling if you find yourself in the wrong job for you. Identify your transferrable skills.
- ✓ Increase your energy level by getting a position you like and doing things you want to do.
- ✓ Get out of your rut - keep yourself ready for promotions.
- ✓ Open lines of communication with the use of feedback.
- ✓ Seek the support of friends who will help you celebrate your good days and help you through your bad ones.
- ✓ Practice positive thinking and seek positive-thinking friends to help keep you that way.
- ✓ Learn how to visualise [not fantasise.] Know how to identify obstacles that may be in your way. Determine how you will go over, under, around or through obstacles.
- ✓ Don't quit when you run into resistance - persevere.
- ✓ Remember that others can't give you a bad day - only you can do that. Don't automatically accept negative strokes from others. Whenever you feel a negative feeling, stop and analyse it to see if you're reacting correctly or over-reacting [which can often be the case.]
- ✓ Beware of 'playing games' which use manipulation to get your way. Deal directly with those you observe, using the same kind of behaviour.
- ✓ Know when you're in trouble emotionally and see a professional to help you out.
- ✓ Deal positively with the energy that's caused by anger.
- ✓ Eliminate anything about your appearance or health that you feel affects your self-esteem level. This could be bad teeth, skin problems, smoking, excessive drinking or eating. No one can do anything about these problems but you. If you allow these negatives to continue, you may be hiding behind your problem, using it to explain why you're not succeeding. i.e.: *'It must be because I'm fat that people don't like me.'*
- ✓ Be aware of your 'negative tapes' and remove them. Replace them with positive ones that describe your successes. Don't accept destructive criticism. Ask others to describe the behaviour they wish you to change.

- ✓ Make full use of ***all*** your talents and abilities.
- ✓ Be willing to take risks and face the pluses and minuses that accompany risk-taking.
- ✓ Believe in yourself.
- ✓ Take the word 'failure' out of your vocabulary. Instead, think of mistakes as a learning experience. The more items you try, the larger your memory bank is of things you do well. Your success rate will rise accordingly. You must give your best effort to make this process work. Don't be a quitter or give second-best effort.
- ✓ Reward yourself when you've done a good job.
- ✓ Don't worry - be happy. Don't take life and/or yourself too seriously.
- ✓ As you're going to be conversing all your life, learn how to express yourself properly. Take public speaking courses if necessary, so you're not misunderstood.
- ✓ People often get tired, not because they do too much, but because they do too little! Get your motor running.
- ✓ Be a leader, not a follower.
- ✓ Success of any kind, whether it is related to money, health, happiness, family, good friends, recognition, etc. is always preceded by hard work. Be willing to work hard to get what you want. Don't expect external forces to give it to you.
- ✓ Define what success means to you, set some goals to achieve that success and revel in being a winner.

'Heal the past,

live in the present,

dream the future.'

Put it all together and you'll have Taken command of your future.

BIBLIOGRAPHY

Berne, Eric, *Games People Play*, Ballantine Books, 1996

Bernstein, Albert J. & Sydney Craft Rosen, *Dynosaur Brains: Dealing with all those impossible people at work,* John Whiley & Sons, NY 1989.

Bramson, Robert M., *Coping with Difficult People,* Dell, 1998.

Cairns, F., *Wife Assault Hurts All of Us,* WINN House, Edmonton, Canada, 1988

Cameron, Grant, *What about me? A guide for men helping female partners deal with childhood sexual abuse,* Creative Bound, 1994.

Cava, Roberta, *Dealing with Difficult People, How to deal with nasty customers demanding bosses and un-cooperative colleagues*, 22 publishers in 16 languages. And

Dealing with Difficult Situations at Work and At Home; Pan Macmillan, 2003, Ankh-Hermes, Netherlands, 2004. And

Dealing with Difficult Spouses and Children, Cava Consulting, Australia, 2002. And

Dealing with Difficult Relatives and In-Laws, Cava Consulting, Australia, 2001.

Dyer, Wayne W., *Your Erroneous Zones,* Harper Torch, 1993.

Keene, Sam*, Fire in the belly; On being a man,* Doubleday Dell, 1992.

Rosenberg, Kris, *Talk to Me; A Therapists guide to breaking through male silence,* Putnam, 1994.

Smith, Manual J., *When I Say No I feel Guilty*, Bantam, 1985.

Tannen, Deborah, *You just don't understand; Women and Men in Conversation*, Morrow, 1990.

Ury, William, *Getting Past No; Negotiating from confrontation to cooperation*, Doubleday Books, 1993.

Walker, Lenore, *The Battered Woman*, Harper & Row, NY, 1079.

Weisinger, Hendrie & Lobsenz, Norman M., ***Nobody's Perfect: How to give criticism and get results,*** Warner Books, 1988.

Woititz, Dr Janet G., ***The Intimacy Struggle,*** Health Communications, 1993

Zimbardo, Philip, ***Shyness; What it is. What to do about it,*** Perseus Press, 1990.

UNIQUE CAREER COUNSELLING SERVICE

AVAILABLE VIA E-MAIL

Provided by ROBERTA CAVA of:

Cava Consulting,

rcava@dealingwithdifficultpeople.info

www.dealingwithdifficultpeople.info

In these hard economic times, are you finding it difficult to find suitable employment in your field of work? How would you like to expand those opportunities? This unique career counselling service will enable you to determine your transferable skills and identify another 20 to 40 occupations where you could use those skills.

An investment of $175.00 will provide you with an extensive report that includes:

- A list of your transferrable skills
- 20 to 30 primary and secondary occupations
- you could investigate that use your
- transferrable skills
- A psychological report that includes:
    - Your strengths in the areas of interest, ability, values, personality, capacity
    - Interest, ability and personality profiles
    - What you think your skills are compared to that they really are
    - Determine your management, persuasive, social artistic, clerical, mechanical, investigative and operational abilities
    - Whether you are outgoing, reserved, factual, creative, analytical, caring organised or causal
    - Your ability to think, reason and solve problems
    - Values inventory
    - Your stamina level
    - Your I.Q. Score
    - Performance and personality characteristics
    - Motivational and De-motivational factors

- o Whether you have what it takes to become an entrepreneur and have your own business

What will happen:

When we receive your payment of $175.00 (along with an e-mailed copy of your CV or resume) we will e-mail you our Career Choices workbook. As soon as we receive your completed workbook, we will send you your personalized extensive Career Choices report. This service can also be done via regular post (but it will take much longer).

To apply, contact Roberta Cava at:

rcava@dealingwithdifficultpeople.info

www.ingramcontent.com/pod-product-compliance
Lightning Source LLC
LaVergne TN
LVHW051519070426
835507LV00023B/3195